Suffering In Silence

To: Sarah

Thank You for Your
Beautiful Spirit
of Healing

By
Andrea Maynard-Brade

6.7.21

Suffering In Silence

First Printed in United Kingdom, 2021

Published by Conscious Dreams Publishing
www.consciousdreamspublishing.com

Edited by Maureen Elizabeth Worrell Dips.Couns CBT BABCP

Typeset by Oksana Kosovan

ISBN: 978-1-913674-45-8

Readers' Reviews

"As a mentor and wellbeing coach, I am always fascinated to read how survivors of abuse and trauma have successfully found a way to heal from their experiences of the unasked-for crises they have lived through. This lady's book, *Suffering In Silence*, is a very good example of how living with domestic violence can seriously affect your mental health and wellbeing and how that type of personal trauma can manifest itself in various and sometimes unpleasant ways. This author's story illustrates that, from a very young age, the seeds were planted whereby she grew up unequipped with the tools to set her life on a different path than that which she had already been taught and knew. The light at the end of her tunnel is that she embraced her awareness of what was unacceptable and decided to change her mindset so that she was attracted to and attracted those things and people that would reflect her worthiness. It is a great read with some excellent tasks for readers to think about and be proactive in completing at the end of each chapter. This is a very highly recommended read."

– M Schmidt, Mentor and Coach in Germany

"I really enjoyed reading this book by Ms Maynard-Brade. This book is very well-written, and the more you read, the more you feel drawn into and invested in hoping her life's journey becomes a positive reflection of all she had to suffer and overcome. She makes the reader feel as if they are part of her circle as she reveals past incidents of domestic abuse, violence and finally finding her own voice. It is a credit that she now uses her past experiences to help so many others, and you can feel her warmth and honesty throughout the whole book. I very much like the added touch of including some self-help tasks at the end of every chapter. This is a book to be read and shared with many others who will certainly benefit from having read it. Well done to the author."

– Trevor Larkins, Clinical Psychologist, Bristol, England

"*Suffering In Silence* is a beautifully written memoir that gives the readers a vivid account and insight into the author's life. In reading her story, we are privileged to be shown a woman of great strength, one who had to fight for survival throughout her adolescence and adulthood. Andrea shows us that she does, indeed, come from a generation of strong and courageous women, regardless if they are silent or outspoken, all of which were in pursuit of peace or calm, despite the fear instilled within them from their abusers. Andrea has chosen to break that generational curse through the trials and errors of her life, but we can see how her faith has never left her. Her citation of biblical quotes throughout her book will bring an extra layer of comfort to her readers, and the reflective questions and tasks at the end of each chapter is an additional thought-provoking and wonderfully constructed element to her story, giving readers the opportunity to think about their own journeys and how it is possible to keep hope alive and improve their situations or experiences.

Thank you, Andrea, for immersing us in the vivid imagery of the beautiful island of Barbados, where, in reading the words, you can easily imagine the exoticness of the people and the foods as you almost bask in the warmth, sunshine, laughter and fun that is illustrated in her story. And let us not forget the historical aspect of her story, which helps us as readers to feel and imagine her life in England in the areas she grew up in, the key people who were instrumental in her personal growth, and the way she describes her family of immigrants who had to adjust to their new life in England but who did not know how to overcome the instilled traumas of their past. It is also to be acknowledged that the author has allowed us to share in her harrowing experiences and vulnerabilities in losing her loved ones. Her story will go a long way towards being the catalyst in bringing positive changes to many lives. Thank you for the honour of being a part of your journey."

– Maxine Palmer-Hunter, Director and Educator, England, UK

"I found it extremely difficult trying to read through all of my mum's book. It is way too emotional for me, as I am reading about my mum and what she went through from such a young age. It was also very emotional and challenging as I can relate to some parts, and it is hurtful to know my mum went through that type of abuse, too. I am so sorry for what that man put my mum through. I am also sorry for those times I haven't been the best daughter I could have been in the past. I love my mum, and she is truly a warrior queen and my inspiration. I have so much respect for her and am super proud of her. I love you, Mum."

– Sara Maynard, Daughter, Author, Businesswoman,
Birmingham, UK

"I have known Andrea Maynard-Brade for over twenty years. I recall seeing her around socially when we were both teenagers, but it was only when we were both in our thirties that we began to forge a friendship, one that has been filled with laughter. Andrea supported me with the preparations for my fortieth birthday celebrations. I have been a guest in her home but had no idea what this beautiful woman had gone through in her past. At times, Andrea looked sad but always managed to maintain that massive smile on her face. When asked, she would always reply that she was okay. In reading her book, *Suffering In Silence*, my first thought was how many Black women there must be who have been through similar experiences in fearful silence. That thought made me feel sad but also proud of Andrea for telling her story. Parts of the book made me reflect on my own life's journey and how easily I could have had a similar story to tell. This book is very personal and shows very clearly the issues faced by many women from Black communities. I found myself laughing in reading some of her story as it reminded me so much of an uncle that I grew with. Other aspects of her story were extremely sad to read, but in saying that, it is an excellent read. The way it has been written, I felt transported back to that time in history, growing up under the rules of the Windrush generation of our parents and elders. Well done to the author who has managed to bring a time in history back to life for many women who have experienced many of the issues that are identified in this book. Domestic abuse is so insidious, and the effects of living through it can take a lifetime to heal, and for some men and women, they will never really recover from those experiences. Domestic violence and abuse can ultimately destroy families, friendships, trust, and that sense of safety and security within the home. It can so easily lead to a lifetime of mental health issues and of enduring other types of abuse. Well done to Andrea for having the courage to put down into words her story!"

– Paulette Hamilton, Hollyhead Ward Councillor, Cabinet Member for Adult Social Care and Health, Health and Wellbeing Chair, Birmingham, UK

"From the beginning you are drawn into the character's world and her severe ups and downs and the traumas that she suffered throughout her life. However, the result of being let into her world, is that you are not only rooting for her, but you want to learn from and grow alongside her. The detailed writing is riveting and enjoyable to read and this is a book that will hopefully help people to grow and become their true selves. I enjoyed reading about the relationship with Mr R and for me, that drew me in further, into wanting to read more of this book. The self-help tasks were extremely good as they involved the reader and were good throughout each chapter ending."

Vanessa Nova-Oviasu. Secondary School Head of Year & English Teacher. London

Dedications

I dedicate this book to all the women who have suffered within an abusive relationship or marriage and who have ultimately come through and survived that experience.

I dedicate this book to those who have truly and unconditionally loved me without intentionally causing me hurt and whom I have loved in return.

I dedicate this book to my children and grandchildren as I want you to know that I continue to grow and learn so that your lives will be freer from any forms of abuse and for you all to know that you are worthy of love and respect.

Last but certainly not least, I dedicate my book, *Suffering In Silence*, to my brother Mark Maynard, who passed away in 2007 and to my daughter Safiya, who keeps me spiritually grounded. May you both continue to rest and rise in peace.

Contents

Author's Note

My name is Andrea Maynard-Brade. Welcome to my personal and progressively healing space in which I share my innermost thoughts and memories of having suffered in silence for so many years. Ultimately, this is my story of having survived and overcome various challenges and adversities in my life.

Suffering In Silence recounts my experience of enduring 13 long years of physical, spiritual, emotional, sexual, and mental abuse within my familial and personal relationships.

I tell you how these traumatic events affected my physical and mental health, and how, with my faith and belief in The Creator, I came through this arduous journey knowing that my life was and is meant for a purpose. It also comes with the opportunity to re-align myself to embrace and support so many other abused and vulnerable women who have gone through or who are still experiencing similar hardships, especially where it has had such a long-lasting and detrimental effect on their mental health and wellbeing.

I hope that my story, my book, *Suffering In Silence*, will enable women and other readers to choose time, self-love, and self-care over physical intimacy, so they can learn to live and nurture their lives in light and love.

As you read my story, I would like you to think about the parts of my life's experiences that resonate with your life, past or present.

This book is not only to share my story, but it is also a working tool for my readers, for them to be positively and proactively enabled to seek further inner-healing of their hidden and suppressed issues and hurts.

My wish for you is that you can all learn how to nurture your inner spirit, to put yourselves in alignment with the universe, your higher beliefs, and your true purposes and passion in life.

Now is the time to give yourselves permission to break free of your physical, spiritual, financial, sexual, emotional, and mental chains of abuse and silence from enforced fear.

Your Health is Your Wealth.

Blissings in Abundance
Andrea Maynard-Brade
Author

Chapter 1

It Was Time to Make a Change

'*Oh, my God! What are my children going to think and become after seeing me beaten, humiliated, and degraded like this?*'

I knew I had to protect my children, but if I continued to live with this abusive man, what else would they have to see or hear?

One of my biggest fears was that in exposing my son to my ongoing situation of domestic violence, would he grow to be an abuser himself?

All I knew was that I had to protect my children, and to do so, I had to leave. I had to get out and quickly.

It deeply upset, concerned, and angered me how my children scattered to their bedrooms in fear once an argument or fight had broken out between him and me. I desperately wanted to gather them all into my arms to keep them safe, but in reality, I knew they were only safe once they were out of his immediate reach, as he displayed his aggressiveness and brutality in no uncertain terms.

They had already witnessed how I had been after he had broken my nose and both of my eyes had swollen with the skin around them turning black and bruised. I had made every excuse not to go out until the bruises had completely faded. The humiliation of anyone noticing my swollen face had shamed me into hiding away indoors, but even then, I hadn't fully appreciated my need or ability to protect them as I was blinded by too much fear. I was unable to focus on anything other than needing to recuse myself from prying eyes or questions. I knew that I was putting up with his abuse because it had been ingrained in me as a child and young girl growing up, which basically taught me to put up and shut up. Plus, the absence of any self-worth kept me there.

I had somehow climbed into that cycle of suffering in fearful silence, but now the time had come for me to find the courage to break free, to break the cycle of abuse and keeping silent through fear of being seen as a victim. I wanted to be different. I wanted to be different and safe. I didn't want to be another member of my family to pass on the cycle of accepting abuse from men. If I stayed, what would that tell and teach my children and their children in the future?

Even when my children ran to their bedrooms to escape the noise of the violence and abuse, they still heard everything: every punch, every slap, every shout, and every sob slipping through my lips. Even through my ordeal, I still heard their screams and muffled cries of being frightened by the severity of the domestic violence and arguments between their mummy and daddy.

I wanted my children to grow into positive and strong role models for themselves, their future partners, and for those around them. I feared that all I was teaching them was that it was acceptable and good enough to wear a mask of happiness, presenting the persona to the wider world that I was a strong woman despite everything happening to me within the four isolated walls of our home.

The excruciating pain I felt after he attacked me once again, hitting me with such ferocity that the bones in my arm were broken, was one of the main catalysts for my having to make a drastic and immediate change regarding *my* home life situation. The fear and shock had held me down for a while, but in the end, all I wanted was to get as far away from him as possible. I didn't want him to be around the children or me. I had to dig deep to let go of the fear of what people might think. I had chastised myself as to why I had allowed this man to treat me so badly and for so long.

I could no longer tolerate, suffer, or put up with his abuse of me. It was unacceptable for my children and me. It was time for me to stop allowing him to control my mind and emotions while hurting me physically. I was so frightened and confused, but a deeper part of me was determined that enough was enough.

He had succeeded in isolating me from my family and many of my friends. It had been that success at the isolation that gave him his attitude of bravado to hurt me whenever he felt like it. I had been so trapped and alone for so long, but now it was time to find my way out of that horrific environment.

In my mother's life, she had already shown me what it looked like to stay in an abusive relationship, and I hadn't wanted that life for my children or me. There was no way we could carry on living our lives with fear controlling our every word and movement. Mum had always taken and accepted everything in her quiet way, but I promised myself a long time ago that it would not be me.

I was beginning to see that fear had no place in a healthy and loving relationship, and his constant criticism and threatening words and attitude towards us were demeaning, and it stripped me of any self-confidence I may have once had.

In addition to having suffered the beatings and being yelled at behind closed doors, he felt no remorse at embarrassing or shaming me in front of other people, which only served to make me want to avoid being around other people altogether.

His violence escalated to the point where he felt comfortable inflicting pain on me with more than his bare hands or fists.

A change was needed because I could no longer bear his sense of aggressive entitlement to have or demand sex with me whenever he felt the need or the urge, despite my obvious reluctance to comply. He would take it regardless of if I were in pain or did not feel inclined to be intimate with him. I cried so many silent tears, even as he satisfied himself without my consent. I was sexually harassed by his sexual demands, and I did not have a clue that without my consent, it was considered rape or sexual assault. He forced himself on me, regardless, showing no remorse in causing me pain or humiliation during sex. He saw it as his right and my duty. He had a way of making me feel inadequate because I timidly expressed my wish not to have sex with him all the time. He sometimes interpreted my lack of wanting sex with him as proof that I was having an affair, and that led to him trying to shame me by calling me all kinds of derogatory names.

I cannot even remember what, if anything, set him off for him to beat me to the point of shattering the bone in my arm. I do remember I must have been holding one of my children on my lap as I clearly recall instinctively bringing my arm upwards to protect my child and my face from the viciousness of his attack. In trying to block his blows from the piece of heavy wood with which he hit me, the impact seriously injured me, and I couldn't move or lift my arm.

I think the argument had escalated over something trivial to do with food, or something like that, as I remember that I was sitting there, eating a bowl of soup.

All I know is that he brandished a large stick or piece of wood in his hands with which he beat me, and the look of pure anger on his face was frightening. At the time, I was submissive through the fear of how he might react, and I would hardly ever answer him back or stick up for myself, so only the Good Lord knows what set him off that day. In those days, I was so quiet, and I would never ever fight him back, verbally or otherwise.

It felt like that particularly vicious attack happened in slow motion while at the same time, it had happened so quickly. It felt surreal and scary. I was of two minds, whether I should allow my body and mind to shut down as I usually did or whether I should remain alert to shield my child from harm and myself from receiving further blows to my being.

He only stopped hitting me when he finally reached the understanding that something was seriously wrong. He carried on verbally abusing me, though, despite my clear and obvious distress.

Obviously, I had to go to the hospital to have my injuries seen and to get my arm put in plaster. I was crying and in so much pain that not to have my arm attended to would probably have meant further, irreversible damage to my arm in the long term. I cannot even remember if he came with me to the hospital, but I suspect he didn't, as he would have been far too scared and cowardly in case they suspected the truth that he was a man who liked to act tough and beat women, and they would have reported him and the injuries he had caused me to the appropriate authorities.

When the hospital staff asked how I had come by my injuries, I lied and told them I had fallen down the stairs. It never entered my confused mind to press charges against him. Even as they were tending to my broken bones, I was in a panic, thinking he would beat me again if he believed I had told the hospital staff the truth of what had happened.

It was snowing heavily at the time, and because of that, I somehow got away with using the adverse weather as an excuse when telling people I had slipped on the icy snow and broken my arm as a result of that common 'mishap'. I even went so far as to repeat this lie to my mum, dad, and brothers, after having to inform them that my arm was broken and after they had seen me with my arm in a plaster cast. I suspected that my brothers hadn't believed me, having been previously summoned by me to my home to intervene in yet another physical altercation Mr R had again inflicted upon me.

I would have been too ashamed to confide in my parents as to the true cause of my broken limb, and besides, my father would only have repeated to me that I had made my bed, and therefore, I had to learn to lie in it without complaints or regrets. I would never have felt confident or comfortable confiding in my father anyways, as I was still holding the grudge, I held against him. I held him responsible for pushing me into this man's arms after he had locked me out of the house for no good reason. If my father had been reasonable and allowed me back into the home that night, my life might well have turned out so much different than it had. I would not have felt like I had no other choice than to go back to Mr R's flat and in short course, lose my virginity to him that very same night.

Once I had been discharged from the hospital and returned home, he displayed a sense of remorse, seeing me with my arm encased in the white plaster. By that time, he had calmed down considerably. I could tell he felt ashamed – or embarrassed, at least – because before letting me go to the hospital, he had insisted that nothing was seriously wrong with me and that I would be all right. I had wasted precious minutes convincing him that something was terribly wrong with my arm. I was always mystified at how he, being seven years older than me, didn't seem to have the capacity to behave better and in a more mature and reasonable fashion.

I had to follow the hospital's instructions and keep the plaster on for six weeks to give my broken bones time to heal properly.

More and more, I had to learn to fight ignorance with ignorance. At times, I would force myself to act crazy like he did, shouting back at him just to see if he would back down first.

It was time for me to make a change.

CHAPTER 2

The Family

M y story begins as far back as I can remember.

In 1967, I was five-years-old, and I can still remember the horrible, voluminous shouting and being so scared and fearful of my father, who was consistently abusive towards my mother.

My mother was beautiful, kind-hearted, humble, and the most wonderful and loving woman you would ever meet. She lived her life for the love of her children, nurturing each of them from childhood into adulthood.

She also lived her life for the love of her man, her husband, my father – or that is what I always assumed, or I could not understand why she insisted on staying. I was never certain whether she loved him or not. I never once heard them say I love you to one another.

I do not believe that my mother was ever happy. She was abused mentally, emotionally, psychologically, spiritually, financially, and physically by my father. She became a broken spirit, one who had lost her inner-light and love for herself. She endured being spoken to like a piece of shite by my father, yet she steadfastly held onto the love of God in her heart. She was a conscientious and consistent woman, ensuring the housework and cooking of meals were completed without fail daily. She was what many would consider a typical housewife. She had been married at the relatively young age of just 19-years-old.

My mother's name is Ralda Forde. She was born to Eugene Braithwaite (maiden name of Forde). My maternal grandparents were Rhonda Forde and Larenza Harewood.

My father, Christopher Maynard's, parents were Ethelene Maynard-Cave and Charles Walcott, all of whom were born in Barbados. My father was also known as Sylvester.

Our father looked after his household, and he provided for it financially, protected and controlled it, and ensured our nutritional health and wellbeing were maintained. We were clothed and ate well, and he carried out his duties as he perceived a man should do, but I am still not sure if he loved any of his children with an emotional intelligence befitting a father who would not willingly dream of causing physical or mental harm to his children.

We grew up *suffering in silence* from the terrible beatings we were forced to endure from our father's heavy hand, yet we had each other as siblings to laugh, play, and sing with to try to keep our emotional and mental spirits upbeat.

Most of the time, it was difficult to understand the reasons we all got such harsh beatings from our father, which sometimes made the lashes of the belt or the palm of his large, heavy hands all the more hurtful.

It is no stretch of the imagination to say that, in the long term, each of us reacted in various ways because of how we were mistreated as children, and I am sure that, like many others, we must have learnt to associate violence with power and getting our own way if ever we found ourselves in sticky situations.

Even as a child, I knew that it was necessary for parents to sometimes discipline their children, but this constant, unfair, and uncalled for punishment of physical harm was not what I anticipated, liked, or even understood.

His physical assertions against his children and his wife would ultimately drive a wedge between him and his children, one that would be difficult to bridge or forgive, even well into our adulthood. Even if he only shouted and screamed at us, it caused us so much anxiety and left us feeling confused and insecure, which only served to minimise our already low self-esteem and self-confidence as young children.

I was the fourth child of nine siblings.

Rosa, the eldest, was born in Barbados in October of 1956. She came to England when she was 15-years-old, but she never really liked the UK. I think she was overwhelmed with having to accept living in such a large, noisy family. She was so unhappy that my father eventually sent her back to live with my Aunt Vera, who was Eugene's sister, and who had also raised my mother. My father later

27

found out that Rosa was, in fact, pregnant, and was the reason she had been so anxious to return home to Barbados. Rosa now has two children: Carl and Leanna.

The thought of our father discovering she was pregnant and unwed instilled such a bottomless well of fear in her. This was why she had been willing and desperately wanted to return to Barbados so that she wouldn't have to face his anger, disappointment, or aggressiveness that came with severe beatings, which would have been his way of punishing her for being pregnant.

I can only imagine how terrified she must have felt, desperately trying to keep her pregnancy a secret until she felt relatively safe back home in Barbados.

Dora was born in May of 1959, and she was always seen as the smartest and most intelligent one. She was quite humble, quiet, and reserved. She attended King Edwards Grammar School in Rose Hill Road in Handsworth. Dora went through her adolescence years keeping her head down and her nose engrossed in books. It had been her survival mechanism to keep out of the path of our father's wrath. Dora took the first opportunity she could to leave home at the age of 16 with her best friend, Lexana, and they both obtained jobs with the Department of Social Security and moved to London.

They had been fortunate enough to live with my father's cousin, Letha, where they shared a room until they were able to get a council flat of their own, leaving the rest of us at home to endure more of the abusive suffering. As I said, Dora was the smart one!

She did well for herself, working her nine-to-five jobs as a housing officer, only returning to Birmingham after having her daughter, Aisha, with the intent of seeking family support.

I am of the belief that with Dora, our father's ear-shattering shouting and aggressive behaviour towards our mother and us as children affected her in that she became far more withdrawn than normal and sort of retreated into her own little world. She must have felt a little safer and emotionally and mentally protected there, where she could at least partially block out the aggression and noise.

Her fear of the possibility that he might turn his displeasure and anger towards her must have left her feeling intimidated and neglected as a child.

Yvette, the rebellious child, was born in November of 1960. She possessed an attitude of indifference whether or not she was beaten by my father. She would boldly look him in the eye in such a way that conveyed her inner-thoughts, warning that she was intent on getting revenge on her father one day.

Yvette was my hero as she always had my back. With Dora attending grammar school, Yvette and I were closer because we were both going to the Holte Comprehensive Secondary School where she gained a swift reputation as one of the bad girls of the school. Nobody would dare to bully me or even to look at me in the wrong way as my sister would have them on the ground before they could explain why they had been looking at me in the first place. She was always getting herself into trouble in school for beating up someone, be they girl, boy, or teacher; my sister was not particularly concerned about her target.

All she needed was the perception of someone saying the wrong thing to her, and it was all over for him or her (or them).

Yvette and I shared a bedroom and believe you me, she often crept out of the bedroom window to go to Canterbury Cross, which was a dance hall located in Perry Barr. More than that, she would bring her boyfriend, Patrick, back to the house to stay overnight. Remember that I shared a room with her, though we had separate beds.

There were nights when I anxiously imagined my father walking in, seeing a boy in her bed, turning livid with rage, and presenting us with the manifestation of his cruel and irate Hitler persona.

My heart sunk just thinking about it.

One morning, my sister and her boyfriend had overslept, and my father had woken up before us. I literally felt as if I had shit myself, wondering how we would get Patrick out of the house.

We heard when our father went into the bathroom, and we hid Patrick under the bed as we waited fretfully for our father to exit the bathroom and go downstairs to the kitchen for his breakfast. The kitchen was located at the back of the house, so we waited patiently for the coast to be clear so we could sneak Patrick down the stairs and out through the front door without him being seen. We knew that our punishment would have been more than a beating if my sister had been caught, and I, too, would have been in deep trouble.

At age sixteen, my sister, Yvette, became pregnant with twins whilst still a student at school. The father, Patrick, had been fourteen-years-old at the time.

I felt somewhat ashamed and embarrassed as everyone at school had been gossiping about my sister. Of course, my father became consumed with rage and had taken it out on my mother, as if it were her fault.

After being instructed to spend the last month of her pregnancy on bed-rest in the hospital, she gave birth to a boy and a girl, and I immediately loved and adored them both. They had been so small, adorable, and beautiful. When she had returned home with the twins, I loved helping my sister to look after them. Mind you, we still shared a bedroom, so at times, I had had very little choice in the matter.

There came the day when my father and my sister, Yvette, got into a huge argument, and he ordered her angrily out of the house. The twins had only been about three- or four-months-old at the time. He had told her that she could leave the children there, but who would look after them if she had done so? I was still in school, and my mother was working part-time. That day, my heart felt like it had shattered into pieces. I also came to the realisation of how heartless my father could be.

I did the best I could to support Yvette and the twins because when I was growing up, she had always been there for me, protecting me, and guarding my back.

Her fierce reputation at our school meant that people warned each other not to mess with Andrea (me), because I was Yvette Maynard's sister, and to mess with me wasn't worth the aggravation or subsequent pain they would surely experience at her fearless hands. That reputation increased when my four brothers followed us to attend the same school.

Yvette went on to have two more boys.

Yvette's display of such unrelenting aggression as a child was, I am sure, a direct influence of her being physically and emotionally abused by our father; indeed, we all were subjected to his fierce tyranny and wrath. Having been exposed to such domestic abuse, it seemed almost predictable that at least one of his children would consider it normal to behave in a similar fashion towards others they deemed had slighted or offended them. The teachers were never going to understand why or how she had, for all intents and purposes, been programmed to respond to provocative social situations aggressively and with a tunnel vision of determination. It didn't matter that in some cases, an attack on her, be it be physical or verbal, had no underlying deliberate intentions, my sister, Yvette, always responded with immediate aggression, determined to have the last word or to be the last one standing unscathed.

I was the fourth girl in my family, born in January 1962. Everyone knew me as Andrea, the helpful one who always tried to do her best for her mother. I was seen as the negotiator who was brave enough to ask my father for what I needed, the one who would help my mother with her heavy shopping bags and the preparation and cooking of our meals.

I was a true Capricorn who wanted to travel the world and climb the highest mountain. I often felt as if I were an old soul living in a child's body. I had been blessed with a wisdom that far exceeded my young age, and I had grown to learn how to be resourceful, especially in difficult situations or circumstances. There were many who misunderstood me, only seeing the tough exterior I felt it necessary to wear to feel relatively safe inside our home and outside of it, too.

There were many who seemed daunted by my stern exterior, but at the same time, there were plenty who took advantage of my incredibly sensitive and emotional inside, even though I tried my hardest to hide that part of me for fear of being used and hurt.

Mum would always say to me, 'Don't worry – you will get your reward in heaven,' but I wanted my reward there and then, here on earth, not when I was dead and gone.

My mum was and still is my world.

I always felt like there was something quite sinister in that house, like it was forever watching over me. I was never sure what it was, but it often felt as if I were being pinned down by it during the night. I could feel its presence, but I just couldn't see it. It was all so weird.

This 'presence' or 'feeling' seemed to follow me for a very long time. I find it difficult to explain properly to anybody else as I didn't really understand what it was myself. I will continue with this and expand on it further, later in this book.

I remember, even as a child, feeling mostly melancholy and low, and I had a tendency to hold onto a slight grudge for ages, never wanting to give in to show forgiveness or forgetfulness to anybody.

In the summer of 1970, at the age of eight, I was playing a game of hide-and-seek in the house with my brothers and sister, Yvette. Dora was cocooned in her own little world, deeply engrossed in reading another book. Mum was in the kitchen, making fried dumplings and fish as she did every Friday.

Thinking I had found the perfect spot, I hid at the side of the cooker, when my mother briefly stepped out of the kitchen to fetch something from upstairs. Hearing my brother coming into the kitchen, I raised my head slightly to see him more clearly, and the next thing I knew I was screaming at the top of my voice as the bubbling hot pan of cooking oil somehow turned over to drip lava-like hot oil all over me.

Mum came running back into the kitchen. Seeing what had happened, she quickly took off the long-sleeved top I was wearing and plastered my burning left hand liberally with butter, which was, apparently, the normal thing to do in such circumstances in those days.

I don't recall who had had the foresight to switch off the cooker, but I do remember noticing that the blue and yellow flickering fire of the gas cooker had disappeared. I never felt such searing agony before, and it took a few minutes for the shock to really kick in.

My siblings nervously watched me from the dining room window as I stood outside in the garden near the gate, trying to shield myself from the sun as it had been a hot summer's day back in 1970. I was sobbing in pain and jumping from one foot to the other, desperately blowing on my burnt fingers, trying to cool them down as they still felt as if they were on fire.

My father was at work on his 2 pm to 10 pm shift at IMI in Witton, and neither of my parents had a car, so they could not personally drive me to the hospital. The doctors' surgery had been closed, it being a Friday evening, so I was not attended to or checked over medically until the following Monday.

I vividly remember how the skin on my hand had bubbled up and how the pus-filled and fiery blisters hurt so badly. There was also this underlying and persistent sting that seemed to penetrate all the layers of my dark, soft skin.

I didn't want to be touched by anybody all that weekend, but my mother bandaged my left arm, and I was so very grateful for my mother's gentle hugs and loving attention.

Early on Monday morning, after my brothers and sisters had gone off to school, my mother took me to the family GP, who was horrified and in disbelief that my mother hadn't taken me straight to the hospital's accident and emergency department. After examining my burns, he informed her that I would be scarred for life. The hot cooking oil had burnt the flesh of my skin off, and some parts of my skin were filled with a water-like fluid in the shape of large, painful blisters all over my arm.

The GP produced a long needle and proceeded to prick them all, one by one. I watched with half-closed eyes as the yellowy fluid spilt out. Mum had to take me to the Special Burns Unit at the local hospital.

By then, my skin looked red, and the edges of the burst blisters had begun to turn black and crusty. My arm was swollen and painful, too, too tender to touch.

At the hospital, they tended to my burnt hand and arm with as much care as they could manage. They were surprised that the blisters had already broken, and there were concerned about possible infection setting in. After they had finished cleaning my burns, they applied some kind of cold, soothing ointment to my skin, which drastically reduced that sensation of my hand still feeling as if it were on fire. They then wrapped it carefully with sterile dressings and sent me home with pain medications and instructions to return at a later date to have the dressings removed and my burns checked.

I spent the next few agonising weeks travelling back and forth to the hospital until the burns required no further bandaging or treatment. As I grew older, I couldn't help but wonder why my mother had not acted sooner in taking me to the hospital, especially as it visibly scarred me for life.

Matthew – the intellectual one and apple of my father's eye, him being the first son and born in July of 1964 – was born after me. Matthew had been the first one of us to get a degree, and he became a journalist. He then moved to London after finishing university to work for the BBC as a sports journalist.

Matthew is an author, and he has written a book called *Games Men Play*. It is the story about players in a top league basketball team and how they try to navigate the demands of the game they obviously love with the pressures of daily life and personal relationships. It highlights how men can behave outrageously with dishonesty, being unfaithful as a part of their everyday lives.

Another of his achievements was when he wrote and produced a short film called *FreeStyle*. *The Guardian* newspaper called it 'a British basketball movie that is a breath of fresh air.' It is a film illustrating the obstacles faced between two lovers from different backgrounds whose love is thwarted and looked down upon by the female lead's mother. She believes that her daughter's lover is not good enough for her, and she stands in the way the ambitious plans the mother has carefully and meticulously planned for her daughter.

Matthew is now settled and married with three children. He continues to work as a personal development and performance coach for individuals who want to bring about meaningful changes in their lives. Having trained with The Coaching Academy, he motivates and encourages his clients to believe that anything is possible.

I would describe Matthew as being versatile, energetic, and driven, always striving to make the seemingly impossible a reality. He has specialised mainly in sports, filming in numerous countries for some of the country's largest organisations, including the BBC and IMG, making and producing documentaries, short films, talk shows, and sports programmes for a variety of broadcasters, including BBC2, Sky, and Channel 4. He was the recipient of the first BAFTA Focus on Talent scriptwriting competition with his piece called 'Honour Amongst Thieves'.

John, the sixth child, was born in January of 1966. John was the one who always got into mischief, and my father would consistently declare that if John had not found God, he was sure that he would have ended up in prison or worse. John was a great football player, but he chose women over a possibly lucrative and fulfilling football career.

John tended to be critical of others, and there was an ignorant tone to his voice, similar to my father's. Yet, John and I got on well and were very close in our thirties, when he supported my son and me after I had split from my boy's dad.

John now runs his own catering business (Divine Cuisine), catering to the corporate and public sectors. He is also a reverend who manages a church. We don't see each other often, and we haven't spoken for a while due to a disagreement over a financial matter, but we know that we can pick up the telephone at any time to say hello and communicate with each other.

We all grew up hearing the phrase that money is the root of all evil, but in my opinion, money is not evil – mankind makes money seem evil.

I often sit and contemplate how many men of God have advised us to forgive, so we must all have it in our hearts to continue to show love and forgiveness to others.

1 John 4 – Verses 7-8: 'Beloved, let us love one another for love is from God and whoever loves has been born of God and knows God. Anyone who does not love, does not know God.'

With this in mind, I believe that all those preaching the word of God whilst living hypocritical lives should remember to live by the laws of God and not by the laws created by man.

I am also of the belief that the Creator takes us into troubled waters, not to drown us but to cleanse us.

Right now, I am going through my own personal and spiritual cleansing journey, travelling my path towards finding my purpose so I can get into alignment with the truth of who I am and what I stand for.

Mark was born in March of 1967. He was the loveable joker, the one who consistently wanted food, and the one whom you could not help but laugh whenever he spoke. He never had a bad word to say about other people. He was a fantastic basketball player and loved sports.

Sadly, he had passed in 2007, after returning home from a trip to Africa. He had gone there to meet his intended in-laws and was bitten by an insect. The resulting infection and disease coursing through his bloodstream caused his death. For a week or so before being hospitalised, he mentioned to his girlfriend that he hadn't been feeling so well. On the day he collapsed, he had gone to church, his girlfriend had made him some dinner, and then all of a sudden, he collapsed in their house. She had to telephone for an ambulance. It was horrendous for her and all of us to watch him go through the torment of suffering fevers, unexplained fatigue, headaches, impaired consciousness, and symptoms of organ failure.

Understandably, my parents didn't initially cope well with the death of their son, Mark.

I was at a barbeque the night before he passed. It had been a Saturday or a Sunday, I believe. I arrived home around eleven in the evening and after preparing for bed, and one of my brothers telephoned to tell me that Mark had been rushed to the hospital. I jumped out of bed and called my sister, Yvette, as she was the only other sibling living in Birmingham at the time. I picked her up on the way to the Dudley Road hospital, and we arrived to discover that Mark was already in a coma. The hospital informed us that they had no idea for the cause of his illness and coma and were uncertain if his illness had been caused by a stroke or a heart attack. They also told us that things were not looking too good for him.

One of my immediate thoughts was about which of us would have to call our mum and dad in Barbados, and of course, I was the elected one to make that dreadful telephone call. I had to tell them that Mark had collapsed, and we were there at the hospital, waiting to hear more information from the doctors. Even though my father was the stricter parent, he started to panic and became very emotional over the telephone. I hadn't the heart to tell them that we had been told that things weren't looking great for Mark. I had to eventually tell them, of course, as I was ringing them regularly to update them on any news we received. The doctors were busy running various tests, and a few members of his church congregation had arrived to lend their support and pray for him.

Mark never did regain consciousness.

I had to telephone my parents again to let them know that their son had taken his last breath.

From the first time I telephoned them that morning, my father had booked his and mum's flight to come to England, and they arrived by the following day. John collected them from the airport, and they went directly to where Mark was now at rest so they could, at least, see their son. Mum was devastated but quiet and humble, as always.

My parents stayed at my home, and the assumption was, as usual, that everything that needed planning and organising for the funeral would fall on my shoulders. My cousin helped me to sort out the printing of service leaflets for the church, and within nine days, my brother had been buried and laid to rest.

My father never fully recovered from Mark's death. Mum, being more of a spiritual disposition and strong in her faith, used that faith to come to terms with it as best she could. She took great comfort, knowing that Mark had been involved with the church, and she felt that his spirit was now at peace. Dad had been more verbal when lamenting over the loss of their son. Mark's death devastated us all, and we all grieved for him.

I had been running on adrenalin the whole time during our family crisis, and it took me a while to properly grieve for the loss of my brother.

I was momentarily irritated with my father who professed to not have any money to pay towards the burial of his son, and because of that, there was no way I could also pay for the professional videotaping of his funeral service myself. Everybody else made it clear they couldn't pay either, so, in the end, we had to forego recording the church service and the funeral, a decision I regretted, to be honest, as it would have been nice to have that video recording as something by which to remember him. In the meantime, my father appeared to not see the irony in his being able to buy up certain materialistic items to bring back to Barbados instead of helping to cover the cost of his son's funeral and burial. Despite all this, it was a beautiful funeral, held at the Birmingham Christian Centre. The singers at his funeral were fantastic, and people from his workplace attended to pay their final respects. The school where he had worked was locked down that day. So many from all over Birmingham and beyond attended.

My parents had been so distraught, but it still did not explain how my father had failed to bring his eldest daughter over to attend her brother's funeral. In the end, it was I who paid the majority of her fare so that she could come over. A few others gave smaller contributions towards her fare.

Even to this day, my father will say that it was the worst journey he had ever undertaken, knowing that he was never going to see his son alive again. It must have been awful for them both.

I had and still have an aversion to not treating the people around me the best I can. I strive to give them the best and to make them feel welcomed and loved when in my company or in my home. There is no guarantee that the courtesy or love I extend to others will be reciprocated, but that is life.

Mark had so loved the most-high God with all his heart and soul and because of that, I know that he is now at peace in the spiritual world with my daughter, Safiya. May they both rest in peace.

Luke, the baby brother, came into the world in March 1968. Everyone thought he and Mark were twins, and they shared the same kind of humour. They were both considered the hilarious jokers of our family.

Luke always took pride in his physical appearance and was a true lover of designer brand names and clothing. He was consistently well-groomed and got away with most things as he could easily charm his way out of most situations with his smooth, placid, characteristic style and chat.

I remember one of my old school friends from Handsworth who lived on the same road as my mother's best friend, and how this friend of mine had named my brothers Matthew, Mark, Luke and John, after four of the 12 Apostles of Jesus, as she could never remember their names.

Being so close and so alike, Luke was devastated by Mark's untimely and unexpected passing. I am sure that he still feels vulnerable to the loss and may even experience feelings of profound grief around the date of Mark's passing.

Fortunately, he had us, his other siblings, to support and love him through that terrible period of mayhem and personal grief.

Luke is now happily married with two children and his son, Isaac Mark Maynard, was born on the 3 March 2008. God ordained this blessing as his child's birthdate was also the birthday of our brother, Mark, who had passed away the year before.

My baby sister, Kash, came along when I was 15-years-old. Everyone mistook her for my daughter as I took her everywhere with me. I loved my little sister, and she was a quiet and happy child.

Kash, the spoilt one, having grown up with seven older siblings, swiftly learnt how to milk that fact but in a nice and loving way.

When Kash turned 16, my parents retired and moved back home to live in Barbados after my father had been made redundant at IMI in Birmingham, the company of which he had been an employee for over 25 years.

My sister, Kash, must have been around two or three when I left home after discovering that I was pregnant. She grew up and eventually trained as a beautician and now has a son. She spent a short time living in Barbados with our parents but now lives in England.

Self-Help Tasks Towards Reflection and Inner Healing

- What, for you, is the true meaning of family?

- What key or life-changing lessons have you learnt from your own family dynamics?

- Write a short piece about each family member with whom you grew up, describing how each of these relationships influenced you, be it negatively or positively.

- Have you been affected by the death of a sibling? If so, how did that death affect you, and how did you learn to cope with the loss?
  - Did you suffer from 'survivor's guilt'?
  - What emotions dominated your grieving process?
  - What advice would you give to others to help them overcome their grief in a positive and authentic way?

CHAPTER 3

'Hitler'

We nicknamed our father *'Hitler'*. We called him that in reference to the German politician, demagogue, and Pan-German revolutionary who, from 1933 to 1945, caused so much devastation and destruction during the Second World War.

My father, thank the Lord, never killed anyone like *Hitler* had done, but my father did sport a distinctive toothbrush moustache, just like Adolf Hitler's own. I do not think our father ever knew this was the name we secretly called him, though.

My father was about five foot and eight inches tall with short, black hair. In his younger days, he always wore a very low afro hairstyle, but as he grew older, his hair began to recede until he was almost bald. His nose was broad – a typical Afro-Caribbean-like nose that spread widely across his facial features.

His given name was Christopher, but his mates all called him 'Sylvester', or 'Sil' for short. My mother always addressed him as Chris, though, and he called her Rose. And what a beautiful flower she was, too.

When our father was around, we had to sit quietly in the backroom in front of the television. We had to remain silent and still. We would hardly dare to speak, and if we did dare to whisper to each other, we were then forced to bear witness to his manifestation of an unjust and abusive dictator of a father when he shouted at us to 'Shut up!' The harsh tone and screaming volume of his berating voice sent shivers down our backbones, causing us to be rigid with fear at not wanting to anger him further. He was quick to unleash his temper but took his time in meting out his punishments, which sometimes felt as if they lasted for hours. I don't ever remember him looking or being remorseful after any of the terrible beats he gave us.

The pain and discomfort we felt after each beating stung our young skins and lasted for days afterwards.

Dinner times, sat in silence around the huge dining table, were always another uncomfortable and drawn-out situation for us children to get through. We were not permitted to say what we didn't like to eat, had to consume what was served up on our dinner plates, and we were not allowed to leave the dinner table until we had eaten every mouthful. If we did, physical and very painful beatings would be meted out with stinging and painfully resounding lashes to our tender skin, sometimes accompanied with an extra-vicious slap across our heads. There always seemed to be an invisible but tangible tension in the air during family mealtimes. It felt more like a torturous ordeal to sit around the dinner table with our father present. It always felt like an inevitable ritual rigidly controlled by him. No matter how good the food tasted, there was never much enjoyment in eating it on those regimented family mealtime occasions.

Even the natural habit of needing to go upstairs to use the toilet appeared to be a problem for 'Hitler', especially if he deemed, we were taking too long up there.

He would stand threateningly at the bottom of the stairs shouting up at us, 'What are you doing up there so long? You'd better hurry up and get back down here!' Even though it sounded like a question, it most definitely was not intended as one. We always knew better than to respond with a reply or an explanation.

Can you even imagine the depth of fear we had to live with? I am convinced those of us siblings who consequently ended up suffering from stomach cramps and pains were as a direct result of not being able to or allowed to do our natural business in peace without the irrational and tyrannical command to come back downstairs immediately!

God help us if we ever had constipation or diarrhoea.

His unreasonable behaviour often caused me to wonder what my father's childhood had been like to make him behave like a brutal tyrant during his adult years, but maybe his own childhood had been of the kind where he was denied love and attention in his own developing years.

I used to spend countless hours wondering if his mother or father, or maybe both, had been too harsh and cold towards him from the time he was a baby or small child. Something had obviously occurred for him to lack the simple parental skills of nurturing and showing love to his own children. It was just too unnatural the way he was so hell-bent on barking after us at every given opportunity and never once asking questions before unleashing his monstrous anger upon us.

Speaking to various family members, I did find out that my father must have felt a sense of abandonment owing to *his* father, Charles Walcott, not being there for him or being present in his life.

Apparently, my father had grown with his mother and stepfather and *not* his biological father. For whatever reason, he hadn't taken on or been given his biological father's surname either. I am not sure if that was due to his mother's attempts to protect him from his or her past. I found out that he had brothers with surnames different from his, too. It appears that his biological father had abandoned him when he, my father, was a very young child, and my father had never really known him, which, for my father, must have been really difficult to come to terms with.

It is clear, though, that his stepfather was around and in his life from when my father was a small boy. My father did reveal that it was his stepfather who had given him the money for the fare to travel to England so he could explore what was on offer for him over here. He expressed his gratitude towards his stepfather for that generous gesture.

Growing up, I never heard my father speak of his biological father, but he often spoke of his mother, whom he loved dearly. He always worked to send money to her back in Barbados where she lived, to make sure she had the finances to maintain her home and take care of her business and herself. My father was also encouraged to buy a piece of land in Barbados, as he was always of the mind to return there in his old age.

Being bereft of his biological father would probably go some way to explain his lack of parenting skills, which, again, was very sad. Had he got on well with his stepfather? Did he grow up with that man resenting him? Was he beaten or mistreated in his childhood? Did he grow up filled with internal rage against his biological father, a rage that, as a small child, he couldn't possibly fully understand? Could that be the root of why he grew up to be so abusive and behave the way he did?

Then again, my mother had also grown up without her biological father present in her life, and she had turned out to be the very opposite of my father as far as their personalities and characters were concerned.

It was clear to see the signs of how my father must have been affected by being abandoned by his own dad. It would go some ways to explaining my father's issues with his almost obsessive need to control others, plus his deep-seated inability to trust people. He must have been affected, to some degree, by his own upbringing and childhood to, as an adult, constantly sabotage his relationships with others. It would also explain his regular bouts of aggressive and irrational behaviour.

When looking back, there certainly has to be a correlation over the past four generations, at least from when men were forced into horrific slavery, beaten viciously with entwined ropes as whips and then brutalised if they were thought to have been too vocal or disobedient. Those slaves were dehumanised and made to feel as if they were nothing more than property, belonging to another.

Those men were originally warriors, fierce and prideful men. Then they were forced to believe they had no right to their anger after being kidnapped and stolen, like so many others from the beginning of civilisation. They were brutally and unceremoniously ripped apart from their loved ones, family, communities, and villages.

How does a generation, a culture, a world of suppressed people ever recover from or learn to comprehend that level of mistreatment and cruelty inflicted upon them? Was the hurt and dismantling of their 'manhood' so profound that it has been passed down from generation to generation? Without the impact of such harsh and unjustified treatment being confronted or acknowledged by Black men in particular, cannot a whole nation of Black males' hurts and resentment be internalised without releasing them in a way that hurts no one else?

My father was of the Windrush generation, and he arrived in the United Kingdom in the 1950s. He was just one of almost a million others who migrated from the Caribbean to Britain. He originally shared a room with other immigrants, all of them desperately seeking a better life. The false promise of an improved quality of life must have instilled in them a sense of mistrust and betrayal.

In 1968, my father had reason to return to Barbados, to bury his mother whom he had always cared for and loved dearly. I had the feeling that he buried his feelings and hurt from that time as he never really spoke about his grief in losing his mother. Instead, he just continued to work hard and provide for his family.

My father was never careless with money, as I learnt the older I became, but we children always considered him mean when it came to money matters. In hindsight, all he was doing was trying to make sure he had enough to pay all of his household bills, feed and clothe his children, and look after his mother and his eldest daughter, my older sister, Rosa, whom he had left behind in Barbados.

He had a steadfast and non-negotiable habit of always making sure to pay his bills on time, as he loathed the thought of owing anything to anyone. This was evident when we asked him for money to purchase a new pair of shoes, for example. His reply would always be, 'Well, you can't get it this week,' but within a week or two he would inevitably leave the money for us to buy what we had asked for. Mum hated to ask him for any extra money, so he made sure to leave her housekeeping money every week without fail.

I never once heard my mother complain to my father about any of the household or domestic bills not being paid, or that he drank too much or gambled too much. It would appear that his family always came first in that regard. Not to mention that he was always of the mind to return home to Barbados once he had retired from working in England. It was almost like from the moment he set foot in England, he had been working his way through life to get back home to Barbados. Maybe that was part of the reason he always seemed so resentful and full of rage. In turn, he thought it reasonable to take his frustrations out on our mother and us. But two wrongs never make a right.

Looking back on our lives, I often contemplate whether he harboured that internal anger of his because he felt under tremendous pressure to look after everyone financially. I mean, who was there to look after him in that way? Still, it was no excuse for his being so abusive and cruelly abrupt with us for no apparent reason.

He worked variable shifts, from 2 pm to 10 pm, from 10 pm to 6 am, and from 6 am to 2 pm whilst employed at IMI. It was a massive concrete workplace where they melted metal, and he worked in the unbearably hot furnace to bring home a wage that was barely enough for his family to survive.

I have to take my hat off to him for that. It cannot have been easy working in those hazardous conditions, what with the intensely high temperatures and bits of hot metal sparking around the place. Not to mention the constant and unrelenting noise and being constantly on the alert for any surrounding danger from the searing heat, the raging fires, and the loose bits of red-hot metal that could so easily damage a person's eye.

My father was a very serious man. He would have a little laugh at times with the family or if he was watching something funny on the television, but I cannot remember many happy times with him at home whilst growing up. He always seemed so morose and filled with a suppressed anger that could be easily ignited without much provocation or cause.

On his arrival home, he would casually drop his work bag onto the table and take off his hat and coat. I don't ever recall him greeting us with 'hello'. We always had to say hello to him first. 'Hello, Daddy,' we would say. There was never the guarantee of a response, which depended on his mood, I suppose.

He had this habit of looking around the dining room to make sure we were all present and accounted for. If one of us was missing, he would ask where they were, and if they were upstairs, they were swiftly summoned to get themselves downstairs: 'What are you doing up there? Get down here...now!'

Most days, when he got home from a 6 am to 2 pm shift, Mum would be in the kitchen, cooking. If it was a 2 pm to 10 pm shift, Mum would make sure to have his dinner on the stove with the plate sitting on top of a saucepan of gently boiling water, ready to serve all hot and nice – we had no microwaves in those days. He would enter the kitchen and say to her, 'Mummy, you okay?' whilst playfully slapping her on her bum. 'Leave me, man, and don't do that,' was her standard response.

He would then wash his hands and face and be ready for his dinner. If it was a 6 am to 2 pm shift, he would have a little lunch, sit in his armchair by the window in front of the television, and read his newspaper until he fell asleep. If we ever dared to make a sound, he would jump up and start on us. When he decided we had been causing trouble, or if we had simply disturbed him, he would slap us with his hand, but most of the time, he beat us with the belt. We nicknamed that belt his 'best friend', as he seemed to love using it to cause us physical and emotional pain.

My dad had a few friends, but he would never bring them to the house. He had several acquaintances he knew well, but he would meet up with them and his friends at the local pub on a Sunday afternoon for a few hours. Saturdays, he would spend a few more hours in the bookies, betting on the horses. He was never addicted to gambling or alcohol, but he did enjoy a flutter or two and an occasional drink.

Our uncles and aunts would come to our house to visit. Three of them lived in Birmingham: Uncle Dee, Uncle Charlie, and my Aunt Cecilia. My Uncle Son-Son and Uncle Burnham both lived in London, but they still all travelled up for visits, and we would go down to London for family weddings and christenings, too.

We never knew my mum's family as they were all still living in Barbados.

In those days, my father drank very little alcohol, which is why I cannot understand why he drinks so much now, in his old age, while living in Barbados. Does he feel free from the heavy burden of having to provide financially for his wife and family now? Now that he no longer has that responsibility, does he feel as if he can finally indulge in consuming excess amounts of alcohol in reckless abandonment and enjoyment for himself? Or is his consumption of so much alcohol a sign that he is trying to shut out his past?

We were all happier when he was not physically present in the house. We took turns to be on the lookout for his return home so we could, with some trepidation, enter into the 'no-kids-zone', which happened to be the front room where only the elders were allowed to go. The minute any of us saw him hit that certain corner of Heathfield Road turning into Leonard Road where we lived at number 130, the appointed sibling responsible for watching out for his unwelcome return home would shout a frantic warning of 'Daddy coming! Daddy coming!' There would follow a chaotic scramble as we dove to secure our places on the chairs or on the floor as if we had been sitting there quietly like the well-behaved children we appeared to be and were consistently forced to portray in front of our father. Despite the anxiety, we all felt at the possibility that we might be caught out, we stubbornly insisted on repeating this childish ritual on numerous occasions. Regardless of the undertone of fright, it gave us a few minutes of deliriously carefree abandonment in a house so governed by so many moments of tension, unreasonably strict rules and punishments, and dominated by our having to tiptoe our way through his aggression and our fear.

I cannot remember which one of us it was, but one day, we were playing in the back garden when one of us flippantly and without thinking threw a stone and broke the back-room window. The fear and anxiety we felt were enormous but knowing that it was where our father sat every night and was sure to see it, we decided not to say anything to him. Even our mother knew about the shattered window, and she said nothing to him.

We all knew that we would be getting a beating that night. There was no escaping from that brutal fact.

He didn't, in fact, notice it that same evening, but we couldn't relax because we knew that the day would surely come when he would realise that one of us had broken the window and worse still, not told him about it.

It was several days later when we noticed how the sudden high winds caused the curtains covering the broken window to blow gustily up and down, exposing the huge, jagged hole in the window. It had to have been at least the size of his fist if not bigger. How he hadn't discovered it yet was somewhat of a small miracle, even if the reprieve from a beating would be brief.

We looked at each other in horror as the breeze seemed to playfully tease the curtains up and down, exposing our accidental misdeed for all the world to see. That was surely the day to protect our bodies with extra layers of clothing as protective padding against the inevitable beatings that would be meted out, and sooner, rather than later.

My father eventually felt the cold breeze blowing in and saw the curtains fluttering unnaturally. After having pushed aside the heavy curtains with some curiosity, he saw the broken window, and his wrath was immediate.

'Who broke this window?' he yelled in his high-pitched, angry, booming voice.

We all looked towards one another as if we knew nothing about it, which only served to provoke him into a deeper display of rage, and he continued to shout at us, swiftly rising from his seat like a huge, black raven, hell-bent on exacting some form of revenge. It was like the broken window had been a personal affront to him, like he felt it was deliberate and done with disrespectful intent against him.

No confession from us was forthcoming as we stood there, brothers and sisters, none of us willing to tell on each other.

My father stomped his way upstairs to fetch his faithful leather belt. On his return, we all shuffled together as my father had lined us up as he always did when he was about to hit us with the broad leather belt.

We must have resembled something like a row of frightened little soldiers about to be thrown into the front lines of an impending war battle. My mind told me that I didn't want to be there, feeling like I was about to face a firing squad, only instead of a rifle, my father was holding a long, thick belt in his hands. There was a look in his eyes which told us that even if we were to confess, it would make no difference. Once he had that belt in his hand poised to inflict lashing after lashing on our small bodies, there was no turning back for him.

I am sure our wailing and crying could be heard from miles around while we each endured a prolonged beating from our father, one after the other.

Our mother stood there watching as she usually did, feeling helpless and unable to defend us against the unmerciful onslaught of painful lashings of the leather belt against our skins, the belt held firmly and righteously in our father's grasp.

That is not to say I didn't used to look at her and wonder why she wouldn't help us by saying something or doing something to protect us from that monster.

We would end up having to go to school with evidence of the bruises and welts on our small bodies, but nobody at the school helped or comforted us either. For days afterwards, it was painful to even sit down; the bruising on the backs of our legs were so awfully painful, they ached right down to the nerve endings.

Deep down, I knew why Mum couldn't help us, of course.

Mum was understandably fearful and intimidated by his brutal and domineering character, and she would often find herself on the wrong side of my father's short and horrific temper. He saw nothing wrong with shouting or screaming at us or Mum at the top of his lungs in an aggressive and threatening manner.

I used to feel so very sorry for my mum. Sometimes, I visualised her as weak for thinking that she could never stop my dad from beating us.

The teachings of the Bible states, *in 1 Timothy 2 – Verses 11-12 to 'Let a woman learn quietly with all submissiveness. I do not permit women to teach or to exercise authority over a man: rather, she is to remain quiet.'*

In this context, I came to believe that my mum was not weak at all, but rather, that she was submissive. It was submissiveness borne out of fright, fear, anxiety, and hopelessness.

In *Ephesians 5 – Verse 22*, it says, *'Wives, submit to your husbands, as to the Lord.'*

All I know is that if my father were to behave like that *now*, he could be charged and locked up for child abuse. In this present era, the law advocates 'The Child Abuse Prevention and Treatment Act (CAPTA) 1974, regarding the fair, ethical and legal treatment of children, which is intended to keep children free from all forms of abuse, including physical, sexual, emotional and psychological abuse.' Given his past behaviours, this sounds like it would have been a very long sentence for my father to serve, and rightly so.

I never heard him complain or moan about coming over to the UK to live, but I think he had a focused plan to come over here to make a better life for himself and his family, and then to return to his homeland of Barbados as soon as he either retired with his savings or had received his redundancy money. He eventually returned to Barbados, built his house, and left the UK soon after everything had been sorted out. He arrived in Britain in 1957 and left in 1994. Thirty-seven long years he spent, working and living in England. He loved Barbados, but I never once heard him say he had regrets about coming here. Who is to say if, deep down, he *did* resent having to travel here to make a decent living for himself and his family, and to achieve that goal, he had had to leave his beloved country of Barbados behind, not to mention his mother and eldest child?

As I am writing *my* story in the year 2020, he is now 85-years of age, and he still has not changed. He is still displaying those uncomfortable and unwarranted flashes of untamed anger and aggressiveness and treating my mother disgracefully.

I still wonder why our mother puts up with it after all these years.

More importantly, what is it that makes our collective mothers believe it is acceptable for men to portray these types of abusive behaviours in front of their daughters, and to keep other women that are known to the wives whilst their husbands continue to abuse them verbally, emotionally, mentally, psychologically, and physically?

What kind of messages do these women, albeit abused and fearful women, think they are sending out to their daughters and granddaughters? They only teach us all that this kind of abuse is acceptable and is to be accepted without question, that it is normal to be treated in such a detrimental, disrespectful, and distasteful way.

Was my mother so submissive and silent for fear of being abandoned by her husband as she had been by her own father? Had her abandonment in childhood left her feeling unworthy of being loved and treated right by men?

Women like my mother – including myself – need to know that they should and can take a stand and leave these abusive men to show themselves and the men, that they are not worthless but worthy of more and better. They need to be bold in knowing and showing that they are not foolish beings, but instead, are very special, unique, and irreplaceable human beings. Then, they must find the courage to leave their sorry asses so that they, the women, can live in peace and joy, safe and far away from the unjust abuse and hurt caused by abusive and egotistical men.

As mothers, sisters, as females, we all need to take a good look at ourselves to notice and to be aware of why our daughters are not married, cannot settle into a loving and safe intimate relationship, and cannot find a way to believing they are worthy of being in non-abusive relationships, inclusive of respect and fidelity.

I don't believe, even to this day, that my father considers his past and present misbehaviours as anything but the norm. Otherwise, why would he continue perpetuating that kind of abusive and corrosive behaviour towards women, and my mother specifically.

Is his increase in alcohol consumption in recent years a sign that he has suppressed regrets and remorse? Does he even think about the past at all?

If I were to ask him, how would he respond to my question of how he feels now, looking back at his mistreatment and harsh punishments against us, his children?

Self-Help Tasks Towards Reflection and Inner Healing

- Did you have a 'Hitler' character in your life? It could have been your father, mother, brother, sister, another family member, or friend.

  - Write an account of your experience regarding the impact of having this type of relationship in your life.

  - How did this relationship affect you, and how did you manage to break that cycle of abuse?

- What are the main lessons you think you learnt by surviving this type of relationship?

  - Think about the positive and negative aspects of such a relationship.

CHAPTER 4

My Mum

Whenever I think of my mum, Rose, I have memories of how she really and truly epitomised her name, which symbolises love and purity and is a reminder to always try to cleanse the mind. Roses belong to the *rose-cease* family of plants. Roses symbolise messages of love, filled with passion and desire.

I know my mum loved her children, but I could never understand why my father treated her so badly over the years.

Equally, I could never understand why she stayed.

Had she been too afraid of being judged? Was she pressured by others to leave, to not put up with the domestic abuse and violence, and therefore, too scared to speak up about it?

Had she believed that, over time, she could fix him so he would change his ways? Had she believed that love would conquer all?

Had her burden of misplaced guilt and shame prevented her from seeing that she was worthy of so much more? Or had she accepted it all because she believed that she was unworthy of decent love and respect from her husband?

Having once been a victim of domestic abuse myself, I know that the hurt and shame runs so deep that many victims go so far as to defend their abusive partners. Some even apologise for their partner's misbehaviours and patterns of abuse and aggression towards them.

My mum has always been so very submissive and always did what she was told by my father. Whatever he said, demanded, or dictated was the rule, and she has never been a woman who seemed to want to go out to explore life beyond the four walls of her home. She was a homely woman.

1 Timothy 3:Verse 1 says: 'Their wives likewise must be dignified, not slanderers, but sober-minded, faithful in all things.'

She was all about looking after her children. Her whole life had been dedicated to her family. She cooked, cleaned, ironed, and washed clothes, almost from the day she was born, but you never heard her complaining about anything she had to do or that had to be done.

She has always been a loving, humble, and caring woman, wife, and mother, but there were many times in my life, as I grew up from child to adult, when I would question her submissiveness and wish for her to stand up for herself, and to stand up to my father. *Proverbs 11:16 says, 'A gracious woman gets honour and violent men get riches.'*

Being controlled and hurt by her husband had to have been traumatising for her, and she must have felt perpetually confused with doubt as to her own sense of sanity, not to mention how she must have had plenty of moments of self-blame and misplaced guilt and shame.

As a child, I could only imagine her weariness and shame at not being strong enough to stand up to him.

My mum was raised by her Aunt Vera, who had no children of her own. My mum was the eldest of seven siblings, and she stayed with her aunt until the time came when she left her aunt and the only home, she had ever known to travel to England to join my father.

She and my father were married in 1958 and are still, to this day, married and together. That is nearly 62 years of marriage!

When she first arrived in England, they lived in a shared house with other people, with the two of them occupying a single room. They lived there for a while.

Eventually, they moved to stay with a good friend and her husband, a couple they had known in Barbados, Mr and Mrs Reid, both of whom have now sadly passed away, may they rest in peace. There, on Heathfield Road in Handsworth, Birmingham, my parents lived in that one room until they had saved enough to pay a deposit towards purchasing their own home on Leonard Road when I was born in 1962.

Aunt Vera was very small in stature, but she was a formidable and straight-talking woman, one who was not to be crossed. She lived in Barbados, where my mum was born, and she was a strong and mighty woman who believed in God. Her faith in God was immovable. *Proverbs 31:26: 'She opens her mouth with wisdom, and the teachings of kindness is on her tongue.'*

She had lost her husband at a very young age to one of the hurricanes that often plague the island of Barbados, and she never remarried as she had loved him so dearly.

She had always been so protective of my mum, and after my mother had given birth to her first child and left to go to the United Kingdom, she looked after Rosa, her grandchild, just as she had done with my mother.

I had the pleasure of meeting Aunt Vera in 1990, when I first visited Barbados with my son, Jermaine. He had been ten years of age, then. From that time onwards, I was a regular visitor to Barbados, but sadly, Aunt Vera died in January 2016.

Growing up in Barbados, my mum had to go to church with her aunt, but even though she had a strict upbringing as a lone child living with her aunt, it was a good life. She grew up loving and appreciating the traditions and cultures of life in Barbados.

Her Aunt Vera was an accomplished cook, and she fed and nurtured her with traditional dishes, such as Cou-Cou (cornmeal cooked with okra and water) and fried flying fish, cooked and served in a spicy gravy, or pudding and souse, a pickled pork dish served with spicy-sweet potatoes.

They would often have what is known as 'bakes' for breakfast, but these were also eaten any time of day, usually with codfish or porridge or cheese. Mum also enjoyed other foodstuffs like cassava pones, home-baked muffins, coconut bread, turnovers, mauby, and bananas. There were so many types of fruit, too, like papaya, mango, oranges, guava, and pineapples.

Back in the 1950s, Barbados was a beautiful place, and it still is. Barbados was originally known as Los Barbados, which means the bearded ones, so named because the island's fig trees, which have a beard-like appearance about them.

They were fortunate enough to live and grow within a close-knit community made up of various other families and many elders who lived well into their nineties and beyond.

The culture of Barbados is a blending of West African and British cultures. English is the official language of the nation, but the Bajan dialect in which it is spoken is an iconic part of the Barbadian culture. The dialect is a combination of the languages from inhabitants in its history.

The vast majority of those living in Barbados follow the Christian religion, with most belonging to the Church of England. There are others who practice the Baptist doctrine of religion. Christians, like Aunt Vera, enjoyed the foot-stomping, hand-clapping, and dancing characteristic of African-Christian religious practices. Prayer was an important and integral part of their lives, and like many others, my mum attended church regularly and every Sunday.

In England, my mum only attended church occasionally even though she had been strict in sending us children to church regularly. I often wondered if that was so she and my father could have time alone together. More likely, it had been because she could go about her household chores and cooking in uninterrupted peace from all of us children vying for her attention and time.

The older I grew, the more I understood and sensed how my mum was a broken woman, unhappy in her abusive and controlling relationship with my father. I could see it in her eyes and body language.

I felt that she stayed because she didn't have anywhere else to go, and there was no other person to which to turn. She had no idea what to do – she only knew that she had to obey him and listen to my father in every situation. There is no doubt that she must have been and felt psychologically damaged by all the years of abuse she endured at my father's aggressive behaviour. She had no say in matters other than her daily domestic routines and household duties. In her abusive marriage, she had no voice, and her unspoken opinions certainly did not matter to my father.

I don't think she was ever happy here, in England, and she must have regretted ever coming over here. I am convinced she must have felt trapped and isolated, with no family to support her. The only friend she had in those days was Mrs Reid, with whom she lived on Heathfield Road, but really, she only had my father to rely and depend upon.

My father was forever shouting and cursing at the humble and quiet woman that was my mum. I heard him hitting her brutally on occasion, but he also mentally and financially abused her for years. Her only choice was to make the best of what he gave her to live on for the house, food, and the like.

I remember my mum leaving my dad once. We – my mother and the children – went to my sister's flat, but even that was short-lived as my mother hadn't the courage or the nerve to stay gone. We all returned home that same day. Back then, I believed my mother had been foolish to return to him, but then I have to think about how she would have coped with five children on her own (Dora and Yvette had already left home by that time).

My father would often berate my mum as being 'stupid' and consistently called her 'an idiot'. She had a really quiet and softly-spoken voice and she rarely shouted or raised her voice. *Romans 14:1: 'Accept the one whose faith is weak, without quarrelling over disputable matters.'*

Mum has always been a God-fearing woman, and I know that it is her unshakeable faith that has always kept her strong. In *2 Corinthians 5:7*, it says: *'We live by faith, not by sight.'*

Mum was quite short – around five feet and three inches, I would say – and by the age of 11, I had grown tall enough to physically tower over her.

She always wore a very short wig over her natural black hair and used Vaseline or Nivea cream on her face. She always brushed her teeth with Colgate toothpaste and never smoked, drank alcohol, or swore.

She was a beautiful mum, and we couldn't have asked for anything more. She never worked until we were all in attendance at school and had some independence and common sense to take care of ourselves and our immediate needs whilst she was out there earning a living.

71

Her first job had been working at British Home Stores in Birmingham as a cleaner. We looked forward to her coming home with the leftover chocolate and cream cakes the shop's supervisors gave to their workers. Mrs Reid helped her to get a job at Dudley Road Hospital in Birmingham, and mum worked there for 15 years. She retired at the age of 55 and finally returned home to Barbados, where she still lives to this day.

Once back in Barbados, my mother continued going to church, and my father never interfered with that part of her life. I suspect it was because he knew that she was praying for him as he only ever went to church at Christmastime.

Proverbs 3:15: 'She is more precious than jewels, and nothing you desire can compare with her.'

Isaiah 53:7: 'Look to Christ who suffered silently.'

My mother, like myself, are representations of those who suffer in silence behind closed doors, too ashamed and too consumed by feelings of guilt, too frightened to speak up or say no more or to confide in someone.

CHAPTER FOUR: MY MUM

Self-Help Tasks Towards Reflection and Inner Healing

- What was your mother like, and how did she influence your thoughts and life?

- What type of mother are you?
  - What lessons have you learnt through your personal journey of motherhood?

- What conversation would you have today with your own mother about your childhood experiences?
  - If there was a need to forgive, have you forgiven, and if so, how did you arrive at that state of mind?

- Do you think there are any similarities between your mother and yourself, whether positive or negative?

CHAPTER 5

The Summer of 1979

It had been a really hot summer's day in July of 1979, and I was
walking home, strolling leisurely on Finch Road, heading
towards Leonard Road in Handsworth, when this man, a stranger,
approached me and started to talk to me.

I immediately felt some sort of connection to him, what with
his aura of male charisma and the positive energy he seemed to
emanate whilst we continued to have a conversation.

I was charmed by his huge smile and pleasant manner. I remember
that I was carrying a book in my hand, and after checking out the
title on the front cover, he asked if he could possibly borrow it to
read. At first, I was reluctant to give the book to him, what with
him being a total stranger, but he somehow convinced me to lend
it to him, telling me that I could go to his house on Radnor Road
to collect the book in two days' time.

I will call this character Mr R.

I made my way to his bedsit flat two days later, as was agreed in his invitation for me to retrieve my book.

After he welcomed me and invited me in, he appeared to be so confident and mature, and he had me feeling at ease and laughing in no time at all. What really drew me to him was his apparent vast knowledge of the world and its Creator. He didn't look or act like so many of the immature boys at school I had known at the time. It turned out that he was about seven years older than I was, so it made sense that he would be far more grown and worldly than I was at the time of our initial meeting. He never once seemed lost for words, always having something interesting to say about something. He certainly captivated my interest from the moment he boldly approached me in the street.

I do recall that a part of my brain had felt grateful that he made me laugh, something that was drastically missing from my life then. He made me feel interesting and worthy of being noticed, almost for the first time in my life.

Having no mobile telephones in those days, we made a verbal arrangement that I would meet him at his flat whenever I could, primarily because I was still living at home with my parents, and if my father ever found out that I had arranged to meet with a man at his flat – and a much older man at that – he would certainly have killed me. Maybe not literally killed me, but near enough for my comfort, so we had to keep our little meetings a secret from anyone who might find out about us. We all know what Caribbean parents were like back in the day!

So, that was the beginning of how I started to see and visit Mr R in the summer of 1979.

I was still in the Sixth Form at school, getting ready to go to college to begin my BTEC in Business Studies, as it had always been my ambition to run my own business. The Holte School was a mixed secondary school and sixth form, located in the Lozells area of Birmingham. It was a non-selective community school, offering students GCSEs and BTECs study programmes plus the additional option to study a range of A-Levels and further BTECs in the sixth form.

At that time, I felt as if I had outgrown the school I loved, and I decided to move onto furthering my education by attending Bournville College in Birmingham, where I would complete my BTECs in Business Studies. Bourneville was a vocational college, and I had been seeking somewhere I could gain the relevant skills, qualifications, and experiences I needed to ensure my future. I also liked the fact that the college was involved in the community, with local businesses and great opportunities with various industries located in Birmingham. I saw it as my next step towards achieving my academic goals.

My father was very strict, so we were not allowed out other than to go to school and afterschool sports activities like netball, rounders, and other summer sports. I was one of the students who excelled at sports and to be fair, my siblings and I were all active in sports. Matthew and John were both good at football. Yvette and I enjoyed playing competitively at netball and rounders. Dora was the less-sporty sibling who would rather immerse herself in a good book, revelling in it and willingly losing herself in the characters of whatever she was reading.

I remember getting into trouble with my PE teacher on one occasion. We had a netball match coming up, and I had the privilege of being the captain of our team. We were set to play a home match that evening after school against another team – Aston Martin or St John Wall, I think – but the PE teacher had banned me from playing in the match due to a previous disagreement. The team was not too happy about it and decided to boycott the match without giving the PE teacher any warning as we had just wanted to embarrass her.

My team waited until the other team had arrived at our school before informing the PE teacher that our team was refusing to go onto the netball court to play the match unless I was also allowed to play.

Realising she probably had very few choices, and her hands were tied, she eventually allowed me to play, and yes, our team won the match.

I knew for certain that I had good leadership skills and strategies, and I knew how to use teamwork to motivate the other teenage girls, so they were determined to play to win.

A few months later, with the school's sports day events fast approaching, I knew I was by far the best at high-jumping, and I decided to get my revenge on the PE teacher, knowing that she was keen for me to represent the school in the field. So, I refused to compete and told her to let Shirley, the white girl who happened to be second best, represent the school instead. This was because we were all aware of how, in those days, the school and teachers used the Black pupils to represent the school, mainly on sports day, but they thought less of us or ignored us at other times during the school term. The teachers knew that we – the Black students – excelled in sports, but their mistake was in thinking that was all we were good at.

Shirley, the white girl, represented Holte school that day, but she failed to win the trophy for the school; she had come second.

Upon entering the sixth form at school, I signed up for the African dance course, and I loved it. It had also served to get me out of the house.

Around the age of 17, I also started dancing as a member of the dance group we managed to form together, and we called ourselves "The Mystics and the Israelites". Bob Randamie, who worked at a probation office on Hamstead Road in Handsworth, was our dance choreographer. The other dancers were Audrey, Verona, Pat, Eileen, and Alex, and the drummers were Culture, Coco-Beans, his brother, Ron, and a few others whose names I have forgotten. We all trained at the Oaklands Sports Centre in Handsworth, which I believe was established in the 1970s.

As a dance group, we travelled and performed throughout the city, and I enjoyed being a part of that experience. One evening, we were performing at the Picture House on Soho Road, and everything was running late. Anxiety began to overwhelm me, and I could only focus on worrying about the wrath I was sure to face once I had returned home late. I knew my father would be sitting at home, stewing in vexation. I barely managed to get through my performance, thinking and worrying all the while about how my father was going to react to my getting home so late. Mr R accompanied me to the Picture House to watch my dance performance, and he walked me home afterwards.

I repeatedly pressed on the doorbell and knocked on the front door several times, but my father refused to let me in. He was obviously very angry to the point at which he would not allow me to enter my own home. My heart beat so fast, and I was scared, not knowing where I was going to sleep that night, but still, my father refused to open the door. My anxiety had been so high, not knowing which was worse: my father opening the front door to allow me inside or not opening the door and leaving me to fret all night out in the cold and dark.

Mr R was hiding behind a tall bush situated at the front of the house, and when it became obvious that I was not going to be allowed inside the house, he suggested that I go back with him to his bedsit to stay the night with him.

I didn't really want to go with him because I didn't want to put myself into a compromising situation, as I knew what most men were like, and I didn't want to feel forced or obliged to lose my virginity to anyone other than the man for which I was saving myself.

All I could really think of was having to face my father the next morning.

I agreed to accompany him back to his place hesitantly, after having knocked on the front door a few more times with no reward of being allowed to go inside.

After we arrived at his bedsit, we sat down to have a cup of hot tea and eat some biscuits. After that, we went to bed, but I deliberately climbed on top of his bed, laying fully dressed on top of his blankets, not wanting to take off any of my clothes or give him any ideas that I was prepared to have sex with him that night.

It wasn't too long before he started to fumble around me and then he started caressing me all over my body. It didn't feel right to me, and I wanted him to stop, but I also felt so overwhelmed by his overbearing nearness that I felt powerless to stop him from doing what he obviously wanted to do.

That was the night he took my virginity.

It was quite a scary experience for me, having sex for the first time. It hurt a little, and it felt wrong and dirty at the same time. I am not sure if I was 100% ready at that time or if it was the circumstance that led me to allow myself to be seduced into thinking that I was ready or should have sex with a man. Throughout the act, I felt moments of anxiety, fear, and doubt. I felt dirty, to be honest.

After it was over, I had climbed out of the bed and went into the bathroom, where I washed and scrubbed my skin with soap and Dettol.

I did not sleep much that night, lying there mostly awake, feeling a little dazed and worried that I had just had unprotected sex with a man I hadn't known all that long, and I felt like I really didn't understand what had just happened to me. I was still very worried about having to face my father the next day, too.

The next morning, knowing my father was on a 6 am to 2 pm shift at his place of work, I returned to the house before he came home from his workplace. I felt anxious as I awaited my fate and punishment.

My mother opened the front door in response to my knocking, and I explained to her that I had been outside the night before, repeatedly knocking on the front door. She told me that they had both heard me knocking, but that my father had refused to allow her to come down to let me inside.

When my father came home that afternoon, he came straight to my room, berating me and shouting about how I thought I was a big woman, thinking I could stay out all night. My reminding him that it was he who had locked me out of the house, how I had been late only because the show's performance had run late, and how nobody would open the door for me the night before made no difference to the argument.

I felt so unjustly blamed because it had not been my fault that I was home late in the first place, and then he had refused to unlock the front door for me, purely out of his ignorance.

His ignorance and unwillingness to listen were typical behaviours for him, so I was not unduly surprised by it, but an angry knot of unfairness had lodged in my throat, and I had to swallow down the rising bitterness I felt towards him.

I was momentarily surprised that he hadn't questioned me as to where I had slept the night before. Maybe he was too embarrassed, scared, or ashamed to hear the answer to that unspoken question.

That same month, I was late with my menstrual cycle and went to see the doctor. I didn't tell my mother anything.

Bingo! I found out that I was pregnant!

I didn't want to have a baby; I wasn't ready. I still had so much to do with my life! I felt sick to my stomach and so disappointed with myself. I hadn't wanted my life to be like so many others I knew who were having babies at such a young age. Two of my friends were already pregnant, and now me.

I couldn't believe it! It hadn't been what I wanted or planned for. I had dreams of finishing college, going to university, and then joining the Navy. Now, all of those dreams were about to disappear, just because of one night. I couldn't get my head around being a mother. I wanted to travel the world. I wanted a career first before having to think about settling down with a child.

I knew little to nothing about contraceptives. My mum had never sat us down to speak about sex, and I know that, in turn, I didn't really discuss sex with my own daughters either; *this has to be the consequence of learnt behaviour.*

'Charles' was my soulmate, and he was not at all happy when he found out that I was expecting a baby. We had been friends since we were 12. Despite his disappointment, he kept a close eye on me, my life, and my happiness, and he showed concern for my wellbeing and safety. He always made sure that I was doing okay.

When I look back on my life, I blame my father for getting pregnant. He locked me out of the house with no good reason or logic behind it, and if he hadn't been so cruel in doing so, I never would have got pregnant that night. I knew soon after finding out that I was pregnant that I had to leave home. Dora and Yvette had already escaped, and now it was my turn to flee that household. I made up my mind that I was not going to be there when my father found out that I was pregnant with child. The way he had treated Yvette and her twins – I didn't want to go through that for myself.

I had to tell Mr R, and he appeared to be over the moon at the news that I was expecting his baby. He didn't deny or dismissed my concern that I couldn't stay at home any longer as my father would be sure to kill me once he found out that I was expectant with child.

One day, I just got up, packed my clothes, and left the family home whilst my father was at work. I never once looked back.

I am sure that my leaving like that broke my mother's heart. I had spoken to her beforehand and informed her that I was planning to leave home as I didn't want to be responsible for causing any further issues within the family home. She was hurt by my decision, but she knew that it had to be that way, and that I really had no other option but to leave. I felt a strange sadness in leaving behind the family home into which I had been born.

I had lived in that house for the first 18 years of my life. I missed my mum and felt so isolated from my family. The disappointment and guilt I felt in myself made me more stubborn and determined to get through the next chapter in my life somehow. There were times that I felt so low that I sat and cried in despair with a heart filled with doubt and full-blown anxiety.

I kept deliberately away from the family house for months, not wanting to see my father. I told my mother that I was having a baby, but my father had no idea.

My father hadn't noticed that I was pregnant until I was about seven months gone. I hid my condition by wearing baggy clothes whenever I went to the house. Once he realised that I was pregnant, he made a dismissive comment, something like, 'Oh! That's what you left home to do!'

In my heart, I knew that becoming a young mother under those circumstances was not what I wanted for myself or my life.

I managed to continue with my studies at Bournville College and passed my BTEC General in Business Studies in June of 1980.

My first child, a son, was born on 28 October 1980. I named him Jermaine Isaac Roberts.

If I had known in advance what I would have to endure for the next 13 years, I would have somehow found a way to put my life on pause because that year is when the real pain began for me.

Self-Help Tasks Towards Reflection and Inner Healing

- Do you remember your first love and how it felt?

  – Did s/he treat you right or disrespect you?

- Take a moment to reflect and write down what you remember most about your experiences regarding your first intimate relationship.

  – What would you do differently today that you didn't feel able to do back then?

  – What was the turning point in your leaving that relationship?

  – If you are still in that relationship, what keeps you there?

- How did your parents react and/or treat you when they discovered you were pregnant at an early age?

  – Write a short account of your personal experiences.

CHAPTER 6

Heartache

One day, Mr R and I had a disagreement which escalated into a massive argument, and he hit me! I was about five months pregnant at the time. I was both scared and in shock and instantly felt despair, knowing I had nobody to turn to.

I ran out of the house and walked the streets for hours. I immediately knew that I could not live with or be with that man and be happy. He had violated me and crossed the line with his abusive and aggressive behaviour.

I remember thinking that he was just like my father, recalling how my father would hit my mother. I couldn't believe the situation in which I found myself, with nowhere else to run.

A total stranger passed me, saw me crying, and asked me what was wrong. I tried my hardest to hold back my tears as I felt stupid crying in front of a stranger. I sat on a wall, he had asked me what was troubling me, and we talked for about an hour, but then I returned reluctantly to the bedsit as I felt I had no other choice. Being five months pregnant, I was too ashamed to go back home to my mother. I felt too embarrassed to tell anyone what had happened, as if being struck by a man for no reason had been my fault.

The shame and embarrassment consumed me.

Mr R was very apologetic once I returned home to his bedsit, and he made futile and false promises to me that he would never raise his hand to me ever again. Even as I professed to believe him and his lies, I knew in my heart that things would get worse and not better. I tried ignoring the voice in my head that kept telling me to run and save myself from further heartache and pain.

Things improved a little, and things were good between us, but that sense of being almost physically pressed down by that unknown 'spirit' I spoke about in chapter one appeared to have followed me to the bedsit. Whenever I was alone, I felt it come on top of me and hold me down. I tried desperately to scream, but no sound came from my mouth.

When we moved to 35 Alexandra Road in Handsworth to a two-bedroom house, the arguments and abusive behaviour continued to escalate.

One of his friends named Archibald but more commonly known as 'Billy', moved in around the corner from us. I never liked him. My spirit wouldn't take to him as his vibes, as far as I was concerned, just weren't quite right. His very presence seemed to encourage Mr R to act more intensely than before, appearing to want to give in to his need to show off in front of his male friends and prove that he was the man of the house and that I, as his woman, would do as I was told. They were all very egotistically driven.

Billy's baby-mother had a daughter and son with him, but the man continued to treat her like a slave or an animal. He bullied, harassed, and beat her into doing all of his washing, cleaning, and cooking. He demanded that she had to bow down to him wherever and whenever she saw him and say, 'Yes, my Lord.' Ricky, Billy, Spears, and Mr R were all in it together, this detrimental foolishness of the abusive treatment of their women. Mr R tried to force me to do the same thing, too, to bow down to him, but they were *not* Lords; they were brutal beings pretending to be men, unworthy of being called human beings. There were people who treated their dogs better than they treated their women, partners, and wives, the people who had to endure the mistreatment and daily physical and verbal abuse. They all wanted to impress each other by acting like the big man, but they were all unworthy of being called 'kings', as they wished to be known.

Billy got a new wife and chose with whom he slept with each night. He took the king-sized bedroom, and his baby-mother had to sleep in the other small, box-like room with the children. She had to clean, cook, and do laundry in that house like a slave from dawn to dusk. I thought they were all mad and out of their minds.

In those days, while living in our house, I spent most of my time in my bedroom. Whenever Billy came over when I was home, I never once felt comfortable in his presence. There was something not right about his personal spirit of self. I knew I was likely more sensitive during my time at Alexandra Road, but all the same, that awful feeling never stopped hovering over me.

Billy took on a third wife (not legally), who happened to be one of his brethren's (friend's) woman. He was certainly given the right nickname – Billy – as he really was a bully; *Billy the bully!*

Mr R's abuse towards me continued, and in fact, increased, especially when his friends were around as he was determined to prove to them that he had his woman – me – under his complete control. He and they refused to see that he was an egotistical bully, an abuser, a rapist, and a small-minded monster who wanted to prove that he alone had the final say in his household.

I entered, foolishly in hindsight, into that relationship, looking for love, happiness, respect, and protection, and not to be abused and treated as less than shite by him or anyone else, for that matter.

I craved a relationship that was all about embracing, showing love, and building a foundation of togetherness, but that man was hell-bent on showing me that his kind of love consisted of regular abuse and isolation from my family and friends. In no time at all, I grew so afraid to show love or affection to anyone, and I was also fearful of hugging anyone. There were several times when I was lying on the bed, hugging my son close to me and kissing his chubby brown cheeks when he rushed in and snatched my baby from my arms. As most first-time mums know, you quickly become quite besotted with your new-born baby, and all you want to do is to hold them tightly and stare at them forever, so his taking my baby away in such a cruel and unnecessary fashion hurt me all the more.

Looking back, I understand why my son would say that, at times, he felt no love from me because as he grew, his father manipulated and conditioned me to leave him alone, even when he needed motherly comfort. He would shout at me to put the baby back into his cot and leave the room, even if the baby was crying in distress. It was so heart-wrenching for me, but I felt powerless to go against his father's demands, rules, and regulations. His father had made the consequences I would suffer if I refused to do as I was told clear.

I was convinced that Mr R had no idea how to love himself, much less another human being.

1 John v 4–8: 'Anyone who does not love does not know God because God is love.'

I always held this dream that my first love would be in my life forever, but as Iyanla Vanzant stated once, people come into your life for a reason, a season, or a lifetime. 'Be very careful then how you live, not so unwise but with wisdom, making the most of every opportunity because the days are evil.'

I was still unsure whether it was something good or evil, that constant sense of pressure, of being almost physically held down by some unknown 'spirit'. I did learn, though, that it would quickly disappear if I chanted the Lord's Prayer in my mind, and I could physically sense the easing of that heavy pressure as it lifted off of me. Deep down, I knew that it couldn't be something good, but the only positive aspect of it being present was that it never once 'appeared' when Mr R was in bed beside me.

Proverbs 21 v 21: 'Whosoever pursues righteousness and love finds life, prosperity and honour.'

Self-Help Tasks Towards Reflection and Inner Healing

- When you reflect on what you perceive to be your greatest moment of heartache, what lessons, if any, have you learnt from that time?

  – Were you left feeling broken and damaged?

  – How long did it take for you to feel fully recovered?

- Write a short piece from the heart, explaining all the above. Don't be afraid to put it all into writing and be brutally honest in your written account.

CHAPTER 7

The Pain I Endured

The next 13 years of my life would prove to be a living hell, and it was only by the grace of the Creator that I got through it.

It all started off well. He worked and would put down his wage slips for me to use to look after our home, our bedsit at number 16 Radnor Road. He would cook and clean, and I was impressed with his wealth of knowledge regarding the world and his understanding of God and life in general.

For the first few months, I convinced myself that I had chosen a good man with whom to spend my life. He took care of himself and was in good physical shape, and in the beginning, he looked after me well, too.

Everyone had been surprised that I was with a man who was seven years older than I, but I was not interested in small minds or boys my own age as I found most of them to be immature and unwise. They seemed to speak nonsense most of the time and have a fundamental lack of worldly knowledge.

Over time, unable to endure the traumas of the domestic abuse and violence, having to suffer the pain of broken bones and punches, I moved out and left him during my pregnancy with my second child in 1981 to stay in a hostel for abused women. Yes, I was expecting my second child with him. During the brief moments of relative calm and normality, we were intimate, and it felt far easier to succumb to his sexual needs, albeit reluctantly, than refuse him and risk being beaten or talked down to. My saying no made no difference to him, anyways. He insisted on having sex and would then roll over and go to sleep, satisfied at having got his way.

When moving from the bedsit we had a joint tenancy at the 2-bedroom house in Alexander road in Handsworth, Birmingham. To speed up the process I had to give up my part of the tenancy agreement after moving out so I could settle somewhere safely and quickly with my child and unborn baby. In the meantime, I had to live at the hostel until the council could find me a suitable home into which I could move with my child and another one on the way.

In the daytime, I would visit my best friend, June, and I only slept at the hostel at night, which was located in Greenlane, Small Heath. The hostel was awful and nasty – what with its low standards of hygiene and non-existent maintenance of repairs, it made my skin crawl. The hostel had a shared kitchen area, and the women living there with their children always left it in a frightful mess, so I could never bring myself to cook there. There was no way I would feel comfortable or confident preparing food there safely for myself or my child. I only slept in the hostel each night because I had no other choice, and I had to prove to the authorities that I was homeless and needed to be re-housed.

That is not to say that I wasn't grateful for the hostel's accommodation. It at least offered me a relatively safe respite away from the physical, sexual, emotional, and financial abuse and aggression perpetrated by Mr R.

The council took about six weeks to offer me a place to live, and I was eventually given accommodation in Winson Green. The area was very rundown, but at least it was better than having to live with him and his violent and abusive tendencies. I knew I could eventually make the new place into a home for my children and me.

At that time, there were several single mums living on Blackford Street, and many of us were from Black and minority ethnic communities.

It had not been the ideal area or the type of house I would have chosen for myself, and I didn't really like it, but at least I had a place to call my own with a chance to make it into a home for my son and unborn child. More importantly, I was physically distanced from harm's way and felt safer away from the arguments, beatings, and the incidences of domestic abuse. In having to no longer live with him, he could not now force me into being sexually assaulted and raped. I would no longer have to endure being forced to have sex with him whenever he wanted it, regardless of my saying no or of his never taking into consideration how I may have been feeling.

Before long, he started to visit his son at my new home.

It consistently proved to be a problem when getting him to leave after each visit. He stayed late and was upset when I asked him to leave. It became clear that his visits were not really for him to see his son but more for him to keep an eye on me, to make sure I had no male visitors coming to see me. Our separation had not diminished his possessiveness or jealousy.

I had only been living in the new place for a few months when I gave birth to my second child, a baby girl I named Sara. She was so beautifully cute and tiny, and everyone loved her and fawned over her.

With two small children to take care of, I grew tired more easily, and there never seemed to be enough time to get everything done. My increased exhaustion meant that my stress levels were high, too. I felt mentally and physically fatigued from morning to night, always struggling to maintain my concentration even on the simplest household tasks that needed attending to.

There were times I didn't have the energy to fight with him about him having to leave instead of sitting in my home until all hours of the night or into the early morning, and I did not always respond to his persistent knocking on my front door. He would get angry and start kicking at the door and shouting abusively through the letterbox at me. I had to call the police or my brothers several times to come to deal with him, to remove him from loitering menacingly outside of my home. His unreasonable behaviour drained me of any energy I had left. My brain felt as if it were constantly in alert mode, but my body felt the exact opposite. Despite the joy of motherhood, I felt as if I were pushing through each day on autopilot, just waiting for my sense of mental and emotional normality to kick back into gear so I could feel more like myself.

After every chaotic storm, there was always the lull of the calm, and we fell into the dysfunctional habit of sleeping together again, and before I knew it, I was pregnant with child number three!

When I became pregnant with my third child, Kamilah, my son, Jermaine, was three, and my daughter, Sara, was only a year old.

Even though I loved my children, and I loved being a mother, the struggle was enormous and exhausting. I loved creating a family life for us, with all of us eating around the dinner table together, cooking together, sometimes having breakfast in bed with my children surrounding me, and just loving our social times and conversations together.

I hated the fighting, the arguing, the bullying, the violence, the abuse, and the lack of respect and love shown by him to my children or me. I often sat and agonised over when and how it would all end, as I could not see a way out from under the constant crisis under which we were living, especially for my children and me.

Self-Help Tasks Towards Reflection and Inner Healing

- How would you describe your 'pain of endurance?'
  - Are you still feeling that pain today?
  - Do you recall the root cause of your mental and emotional pain?

- Have you ever experienced abuse from another person?
  - Were you raped or sexually assaulted?
  - How did you cope or deal with the experience?
  - Have you ever sought counselling for your traumatic experience(s)?
  - In your experience, did the police or any other authorised organisation(s) assist you?

CHAPTER 8

Winson Green Our Sisterhood Community

Winson Green was a happy little community with a lot of single mums watching out for each other. It was seen as the informally defined inner-city area located in the west of the city of Birmingham. It was also the location of the HM Prison Birmingham and of the City Hospital, as well as the All Saints Hospital building. Most of that area was built on sandy, pebbled soil, which had formerly been heathland, covered in tall, tough grass with bushes and a few small trees. Winson Green lay roughly between Dudley Road and Soho Road. Back in the day, it was considered a good agricultural development opportunity, when, as was common with several other heaths, it had been enclosed. The 'green' of Winson Green lay near the junction of Winson Green Road and Handsworth New Road. Back in the late 1760s, I believe, there was a canal that cut through the Southern part of the Heath.

In the middle of the nineteenth century, land was at its premium, and a large part of the Heath was used to build the borough's prisons, a lunatic asylum, workhouses, and fever hospitals. The area was built up primarily with working-class housing, which joined urban developments from Smethwick and Handsworth. By that time, the name Winson Green no longer referred to just a location but rather, to the district covering most of the former Birmingham Heath. To this day, I do believe that Victorian streets are still there, along with the surviving Victorian buildings that have been around for so many years.

Just as more and more families flocked to the area, so, too, did the prison population grow.

Winson Green Prison was one of its first great developments on Winson Green Road, with its entrance designed to resemble the gatehouse of a medieval castle. Over time, it was expanded to hold some 1,400 male prisoners, mainly those on remand and trial, but it also occupied four wings for sentenced Category B and C prisoners.

At the same time as the prison was being built, nearby on Lodge Road, the Borough Lunatic Asylum was being constructed with a walled farm erected next to it to provide a healthy, open-air working area for patients. There have obviously been many an extension built to it over the years, and it was used as All Saints Hospital up until around 2000 when new hospital buildings were built. The old main building, built in 1883, still stands, and the original east buildings were used for smallpox and scarlet fever patients.

On Dudley Road with its entrance on Western Road, the Birmingham Union Workhouse was built around the same time, too. It was a Tudor-style building, originally built to house around

1,100 inmates, but in all reality, by 1881, its population had double that number. Extreme poverty led to various illnesses and much of the workhouse was gradually taken over by sick wards. Today, only the entrance lodge survives, labelled as the so-called 'Gateway of Tears', and this, too, is currently out of use. It was renamed and re-used as the Dudley Road Hospital around 1922, and a larger extension was opened in 1966 to house the casualty and out-patient department. There is a bronze statue there on its wall, made in 1968, which is two-times life-sized, called 'Compassion', which depicts a mother with outstretched arms guiding her child's first steps.

Despite living with and having to deal with abusive male partners, we women residing on Winson Green tried our best to have each other's backs. We all knocked on each other's doors for milk and sugar or to babysit each other's small children or babies. From time to time, the abusive men appeared in our lives to cause havoc and upheaval in the neighbourhood. The police would be called, but they did very little to help us.

I often find myself in situations where I had to reach desperately out to my four brothers to come to rescue me whenever Mr R became extremely abusive, as I was becoming more and more afraid for myself and my children. There were times when he seemed out of control in his aggression towards us.

There was no way of talking to him when his ignorance was at its peak, not to mention his aggressive and angry temper, which tended to overshadow any form of rationality. My brothers would *try* to talk to him and calm him down, but he continued to use me as a punching bag. I had to constantly find ways to hide my bruises from prying eyes and the outside world. I felt degraded, worthless, and dirty, especially when he forced me to have sex with him, a despicable act in which he was never gentle, kind, or considerate.

Whenever he was upset, everything was blamed on me and became my fault!

I tried to take steps to protect myself and my children, but he sabotaged all of my attempts to do so. I constantly battled against how feeble, vulnerable, and exposed he left me feeling. It felt as if I had no choice but to suffer his beatings causing me physical harm.

I signed up to take karate lessons, but Mr R became concerned and wary that I would excel in this and potentially, as a result, defend myself and harm him instead, so he deliberately turned up late to look after the children so I could not attend my karate lessons. It meant that I often missed my training classes. I had to give them up in the end as I had no other family around me to step in to support me at the time. His continued sabotage of the steps I was trying to take to protect myself and my children from his abuse, and in turn, trying to better myself, left me feeling resentful, and at times, so hopeless, despondent, and depressed.

After the birth of my third child, I wanted a three-bedroom house so my children and I could grow into the space and gain more stability for our future. I also wanted to move to escape the constant embarrassment I felt as Mr R continued to come around, causing arguments to the point where the police were regularly at my front door. I couldn't shake the shame I felt in having the neighbours and surrounding community know my dreadful personal business regarding how I was becoming another domestic violence statistic, a woman who appeared to have no other alternative than to put up with her partner regularly abusing her without having to face the consequences of his terrible actions.

At the time, I am not even sure if I took time out to acknowledge or fully understand the full impact of being consistently verbally, emotionally, physically, and sexually violated by him. All I remember is this overwhelming sense of feeling distressed, fearful, and at times, isolated and hopeless. I clearly recall feeling trapped by the seemingly never-ending cycle of being attacked.

There were times when I felt like I was coping and dealing quite well, but other times, I felt as if the whole burden of having to endure and cope was just too much. Times when I felt depressed and lonely and filled with shame, embarrassment, and guilt only meant that my anxiety and lack of proper sleep had grown out of control.

At times, I felt so off-balance in my life to the point of feeling numb or suddenly alert and panic-stricken. I was confused by my varying reactions and responses to being abused or even by the memory of it. There were occasions when I barely had time to fully recover from one incident before there was another onslaught of violence perpetrated against me.

Everything I experienced slowly eroded my self-esteem and self-confidence, and there were times when I experienced moments of self-hate, too. A huge part of me was beginning to fear being around new people more and more and of being engaged in any type of personal relationship with another person.

I was fearful of confiding my experiences to anyone else as I was convinced they would tell me to just get on with it, which would have only left me feeling more ashamed, isolated, and devastated.

Having Mr R constantly in and out of my life and the lives of my children only served to decrease how safe I felt and gave me no room in which to try to heal, either physically, emotionally, or from within in a spiritual sense.

I felt like my choices were decreasingly limited as to what I could do to escape his abusive clutches, especially after realising that I had no external help upon which to fully rely. I knew that others wouldn't understand because at times I didn't understand it myself, especially with him blaming me for everything bad he had ever inflicted on me or anything that personally upset him. My shame and guilt forced me to remain silent, made me want to keep the abuse a secret, and wrongly believe it had been all my fault that he had chosen to abuse me for no apparent reason.

Frequently, I found myself doubting people more and more, and I scolded myself repeatedly for trusting them too easily. It was like my personal compass refused to work in terms of judging who was safe to be around and who was not.

I reached a devastatingly low point where I couldn't feel comfortable or confident enough to trust my own thoughts and feelings anymore. I certainly had no inkling of ever seeing any light at the end of the very long and dark tunnel that seemed to loom depressingly ahead of me. I remember feeling like I had no right to hope or wish for more than I was experiencing or living through.

Other times, the anger of my lived experiences left me feeling so angry and pissed off that all I could think about was how much more I deserved, not only for me but also for my children.

It would take me years of heartache and suffering in silence before I learned the importance and empowerment of trusting and respecting the ways of coping that allowed me to at least survive and protect myself mentally and physically.

After the terrible Handsworth riots in December 1986, the government introduced a scheme where people of colour were to be appropriately housed. I think there was some type of court of appeal situation whereby it was found that the Right to Rent Scheme, a key aspect of a hostile environment, was a direct or indirect cause of racial discrimination. It was confirmed that as a result of this scheme, it proved more difficult for black people, ethnic minorities, and migrants to rent a home than it was for white British people. This was inclusive of discrimination in the housing market against British people of an ethnic minority, such as the Windrush generation.

Even though it was common sense to see how any degree of racial discrimination was unacceptable, the courts stopped short of actually ruling that the Right to Rent Scheme violated the human rights of law, leaving it up to members of parliament and the government to decide whether racial discrimination was 'greater than envisaged'.

This all happened at a time in which I felt that my own life and those of others like me, those who suffered from domestic abuse in silence behind firmly closed doors, whose lives depended on their ability to stay at home safely, had been dismissed. I felt somewhat let down and disregarded that as individuals and families from ethnic minorities – such as myself – we were being forced by the government to face discrimination and unnecessary obstacles to find a safe place for us and our families to live.

Desmond Jaddo, a housing officer at the time, assisted me in my application for a house, and I was eventually offered a three-bedroom property. The house was situated close to where Mr R's mother lived. Fortunately for me and my current situation, I always got on very well with her.

Self-Help Tasks Towards Reflection and Inner Healing

- What is your personal understanding of 'sisterhood'?

  – Do you feel connected to your own tribe of 'sisters'?

- Write a short poem about what having a network of like-minded women in your life means to you.

CHAPTER 9

When My Baby Died, I Nearly Died Too

I was 27 years of age, it was 1989, and I was pregnant with my fourth child.

Yes, number four! You may well be wondering right now if I were crazy or what, if I would never learn, and whether I was ever going to stop having children with him and just leave him. Believe me: I often thought that myself.

Years flew by, and I felt that I was forever going around in circles, still trapped in that toxic relationship, constantly arguing in front of the children. What with the mental abuse and him making me feel humiliated whenever other people were around us, I only had to say something – anything – and he would shout at me to shut up! I would be so embarrassed, not knowing where to look when, suddenly, all eyes would be on me, whether in sympathy, embarrassment, or fear of what might transpire next. He loved to show off and treat me badly in front of his friends, embarrassing me when we were at home. He would call me down from where I was upstairs just to come to make him and his friends' drinks when he could have clearly done so himself. He was hell-bent on proving to his *brethren*, as he called them, that he was in charge.

That sense of entrapment surrounded me, kept me living on edge and filled with anxiety, nervousness, and fear most of the time. I felt so drained and trapped.

People kept calling me '*Smiler*', but it was the last thing I felt like doing.

Proverbs 14 – Verse 13: 'Laughter can conceal a heavy heart, but when the laughter ends, the grief remains.'

I did not talk much to other people, but I always forced a smile on my lips to mask the burdensome pain and hurt I experienced and suffered in lonely silence. There were only a few family members and close friends who knew how unhappy I was, but deep inside, I hurt and cried out for help to escape my nightmare of a life.

As determined as I was, I continued working hard with my studies, still attending college to gain my National in Business Studies Certificate (BTEC), with the aim of keeping my mind focused and silencing the negative thoughts that bothered me most days as it had not been all doom and gloom. We experienced some good days and times together.

Continually feeling as if I wanted to better myself, and I began reading more inspirational books and the Bible. I desperately sought out love and peace in my life, but it never came, avoiding me as if I were the plague. I couldn't help but think that I was born to suffer, to be miserable and unloved. I became convinced that I would never be loved in the way I so desired. Back in those days, the older generations used to say that if a daughter looked too much like her mother, she was born for bad luck. Well, that must have been me because I am the spitting image of my mother.

I convinced myself that the more I read or watched images of others living happy and carefree lives it would somehow rub off on me, and I would be like those couples on television who were so in love and always laughing and enjoying life.

I learnt how to apply the techniques of visualisation, a skill used to create images, diagrams, or animations to communicate a message to yourself or others, basically using your imagination to its fullest level or potential.

Absorbing it all, I listened to positive affirmations, watched Oprah on television, and never missed an episode.

I read and studied *The Secret*, written by Rhona Byrne, and I wrote down copious notes after reading Iyanla Vanzant's written words of motivation and inspiration.

I questioned myself as to why me? Why had I not attracted happiness and fallen in love with someone who would see me as worthy, too? Why could I not find happiness and be successful in what I wanted to do?

I completed my course in June of that year and felt somewhat relieved to have at least a full month's rest before my baby was due to be born.

After losing my expected fourth child to a stillbirth, still feeling so caged-in with no possible way out, I chastised myself as to how I could possibly have allowed myself to become pregnant again with that abusive man. Why hadn't I thought about using contraceptive protection is beyond me now, even though I hated the thought of using any artificial forms of protection, such as the contraceptive pill or any other pharmaceutical aids to avoid pregnancy.

I vividly remember the circumstances leading up to how I lost my baby. It had been Friday the 18, and after I had finished cooking some fish and dumplings, we all ate.

The following day, I woke up feeling really unwell and started to vomit, having to run from the bedroom to the bathroom next door.

Mr R and the children were at home, and I had to sit up in bed with a pillow behind my head, afraid to lie down in case that terrible feeling of nausea and sickness returned. Later that afternoon, Mr R indicated that he wanted to 'Go out the road,' as that is how they spoke in those days, and I struggled out of my bed, and the children and I got ourselves ready. He then took us down the road to where his mother lived, which was literally a drive of no more than two minutes away.

Upon arriving at his mother's house, I sat down in a chair, and his mother was in the kitchen, cooking as she so loved to do.

I continued to feel nauseated, which, as I had begun to realise, could have been the result of food poisoning. This was accompanied by bouts of gastrointestinal distress, which, as you might have guessed, was diarrhoea. I just wanted to go back home, but Mr R informed me that he would only be about an hour. He didn't return until well after two hours had passed. I was so upset as he had known that I was feeling ill. He and the children ate, and then we returned home, where the sickness continued for the duration of the evening.

The vomiting and loose bowels continued to the point where I had to call the emergency GP. My GP, Dr Misra of the Soho Road Surgery, was unavailable, so they sent a locum doctor who gave me some sachets to drink to try to stop my diarrhoea and vomiting, but they didn't help me at all. If anything, my symptoms had worsened, and I felt worse than before.

Mr R was a part-time DJ at a club, and it being Saturday night, he had gone to play there. Well, I would say that he *chose* to go to play, knowing full well that I was sick and had three small children at home to look after, even though they had fallen asleep by then. His behaviour just proved to me how some men are no good and will put music and their needs before health and wellbeing, not to mention the unborn child I was carrying for him.

He dressed and left for the club around nine that night. I pretended that I was feeling fine as I knew he wanted to go. We didn't live far from the Finch Road Club where he played with Big Belly P on the weekends. Mr R popped back to the house every hour or so to check that I was doing and feeling okay, as in those days, we didn't have mobile phones as a way of communicating with one another. I sat there, upright in the bed all night long, too afraid to put my head down on the pillow. Early on the next day, I felt terribly sick and weak. I eventually telephoned the hospital's maternity ward, and they organised for an ambulance to collect me as they were concerned that my unborn baby and I could be in medical danger. Once the ambulance arrived, I was so weak that I couldn't even get out of the bed unassisted. The paramedics had to carry me down the flight of stairs, strapped securely into a medical chair they carried into the house from the back of the ambulance.

Once I arrived at the Dudley Road hospital, they took my blood pressure and temperature immediately and monitored the baby's heartbeat.

The baby-heart-monitoring machine was quiet; there was nothing, no movement and no heartbeat echoing from the machine.

I was in shock and disbelief. I kept telling myself that she would be all right, that it was some sort of mistake, but to my utter dismay, my baby, Safiya, did not make it. She died of stillbirth.

I could not believe this was happening to me.

After losing my expected fourth child to a stillbirth when I was 35 weeks into my pregnancy, I also almost lost my own life as well. Complications had set in involving the placenta, where its blood supply had not functioned properly, and there was, therefore, not enough blood supply reaching my unborn child in my womb. With the lack of nutrition, my baby should have been getting, my baby had little chance of surviving.

The doctor explained to me about a condition known as pre-eclampsia, which causes acute high blood pressure. As a result, I lost my baby due to food poisoning and the severe diarrhoea and vomiting I suffered. The illness caused my body to lose massive amounts of fluid, making me dehydrated and causing fluids to build up in my brain. Had the fluid drained from my brain, I would not be here today to tell my story.

That illness, known as hydrocephalus, resulted in increased pressure in my brain, which the doctors explained was dangerous and could be fatal. I was lucky I did not suffer any lasting brain damage or convulsions (the www.nhs.uk website explains it better than I ever could). It was a horrendous and frightening time for me.

There are some stillbirth organisations that can help and support mothers through this ordeal of sadness and the loss of their baby or babies, organisations such as *The Lily Mae Foundation* and *MEND (Mommies Enduring Neonatal Death)*.

My best friend, June, was there with me, as she had been with the births of all of my children. Mr R kept coming in and out of the room where I was constantly monitored and observed by the midwives. There was nothing any of the medical staff could do for me other than to help and support me in having my baby without a caesarean operation. One of the midwives had broken my waters to stimulate my labour, so I could deliver her naturally through the vaginal birth canal. After she had been delivered, I had held her close to me, hoping and praying that she would wake up, but to my dismay, she didn't. My heart sunk even though I tried not to show my devastation. I just kept thinking that I had to be strong for my three surviving children. There was no way I could allow myself to break down or to give in to my suppressed desire to scream and sob out loud.

After the very sad and painful funeral for my beautiful baby, Safiya, (her name meant 'pure, sincere friend' in Arabic), I tried to seek out and gain clarity about where I needed to go with my life. I needed to look within to see why my life was always so painful and so awful to bear and live. I needed to survive to find true love to validate my suffering of all the pain and heartache.

Safiya father arrived at the church dressed in a pair of jeans! I wasn't pleased, but after seeing the little white coffin, I crumbled inside. The pain felt so deep inside of me that I was overwhelmed. I fought back the tears threatening to escape and pour down my face just to appear brave in front of everyone there.

I needed to seek and gain clarity about where I needed to go with my life. I don't remember how long it took me to recover from the grief, as losing a baby to stillbirth is incredibly painful. I cannot explain the pain, and my emotions were all over the place, yet I kept it together with that mask pasted firmly in place.

Grief is so personal and unique to every individual, and it can affect all of us in different ways. I felt guilty, thinking to myself about the possibility of what I might have done wrong and what I could have done better or differently. I tortured myself, thinking about how I could have eaten something that had harmed the baby inside of me.

If only the locum doctor had sent me to the hospital earlier when I had first called him out that night, would things have been different? Could his lack of not doing more for me be seen as negligence on his part? Could I have insisted that I needed further medical advice and help than I had initially received?

I felt so lost, sad, and alone. My heart literally felt broken into unfixable pieces. I felt as if I had died, too, along with my baby, and I was overwhelmed with a deep sense of sadness and depression. I had to look within to see why my life was always so painful, so awful to bear. All I knew was that I had to somehow survive to find true love to validate my suffering of all the pain and heartache. I felt overwhelmed, with a deep sense of sadness and loneliness and no help or support from the doctors or counsellors. There had been nothing. It was only the help and support of my closest friends that had seen me through that horrible time of having to grieve for my beautiful baby daughter.

I also had a sense of relief that my baby hadn't survived to be brought into this world to live this frightful, negative life I was experiencing with her siblings. That didn't stop me from weeping in secret, though, away from prying eyes and utterances of well-intentioned and comforting words. I knew these words were spoken out of concern, but they didn't soothe the deep hurt and loss I had felt at the loss of my baby girl.

I closed my eyes in prayer every day as I sought peace for myself and thanked The Most High God for having taken her to a safer place. I gave thanks that she was now resting in peace and free from harm and any emotional upheaval.

I felt thankful I could still feel her love and presence around me. I sensed, with a grateful heart, that she never really left me. She would always be there to love and protect me, sending me the scent of lavender to remind me that she was still there in the spiritual world and still close by. The tears still pour from my eyes every time I think of or visualise those moments when I know she is watching over me. I will always love her so much.

After that close call with death, I was forced to start reflecting on my life in a serious way. I felt suffocated in the abusive relationship and needed to get out of it. I also felt that I couldn't just walk out, but I knew it was fear and self-doubt that kept me there.

I was so confused and scared as to what to do for the best.

You know that song by Elvis Presley, *Suspicious Minds*? The lyrics kept ringing in my head like a thunderous warning to get out and never look back.

I couldn't fully understand what was stopping me from just running away and leaving him for good. It wasn't as if I had any love for him in my heart anymore. I can honestly say that I hated him and my life with him. Maybe I stayed because of the unconditional love I had for my children; I wasn't sure. All I knew was that I was devastated as I felt like I was becoming the woman my mother was, the kind of abused, submissive woman I had always promised myself I would not become. Well, no – not on my watch! As Lisa Nichols would say.

As time went on, I began to realise that abuse within a relationship does not get better unless you do something about changing it.

I didn't know what to do, and the frustration of it all was taking its toll on me. Things were just getting worse. I had nowhere to go. The police were of little help. My family couldn't be my personal security, 24 hours a day. I felt so emotionally and mentally disconnected from everyone around me.

I had to find a way to use the strength and compassion within me to love and trust myself enough to get out of the vicious cycle of domestic abuse. I prayed to my ancestors for guidance to break the generational curses of being abused and accepting it as normal.

Mr R tried his hardest to isolate me from my family and friends. I hadn't known it at the time, but this is what prolific abusers do. It is their twisted way of trying to feel powerful and in control.

I wasn't allowed to go out with my friends, but I remember one occasion where he had said I could go out with the girls. I spent that day doing all the washing, cooking, and cleaning so there would be no excuses or issues for him to use against me to prevent me from going out. I made doubly sure that he was happy and calm that day.

When my friends arrived, I was upstairs getting ready. I had been feeling both anxious and excited to have been allowed out, even for a little while, after being held prisoner in my own home for so long.

As I came down the stairs, all dressed and ready to go, he suddenly switched his mood and declared to all of us standing there, 'You know something? You are not going nowhere!'

My heart sunk and plummeted to my feet.

He wouldn't budge despite my friends' begging him to let me go out with them. He would not change his mind at all. In the end, my friends left and went to the party without me.

I was so angry and humiliated that I had cried myself to sleep, as I did most nights.

More than ever, it was clear that I was a prisoner in my own home and had no freedom to go out without his permission. I was tired of being dictated to, slapped around, punched, and forced to have sex with a man I detested.

The depths of humiliation I felt were so deep that it was as if I were being sucked into a never-ending well of despair.

I was both angered and bewildered by his apparent inflated and exaggerated sense of self-importance and power over me and who I saw and what I did or didn't do.

His expectation of being recognised as my superior, even without any particular achievements to warrant it, left me feeling resentful and filled with a rage that I had no way to vent without bringing his anger down on my head or body.

He possessed this grandiose sense of egotism and self-importance that left me feeling more and more befuddled and uncertain of myself, and I was left doubting what the right or safe thing to think, say, or do was.

I had grown weary of his need to constantly belittle, demean, intimidate, and bully me into submitting to his ever more illogical demands and instructions. With each day that passed, I felt that he was increasingly exploiting my vulnerabilities and my fear of him and his explosive temper.

Because of his lack of understanding and empathy, I convinced myself that nobody else would understand or sympathise with my situation either, which meant that I withdrew further into myself and further into my quietness, being fearfully and hopelessly silent.

He manipulated me to the point where I believed him in thinking that he had become so important in my life that I couldn't possibly survive or function without him by my side or in my life.

I had been blind to his disdainful and patronising way of speaking to me and how he mistreated me for so long. His inflexibility became jarring and nauseating to me, intruding into every part of my thinking and being. His misbehaviours and abuse of me only caused me distress and hours upon hours of shedding tears of frustration when I was alone.

Up until the death of my fourth child, I had never taken any contraceptive pills, and he hadn't liked using condoms, like most black men, in those days. A lot of those black men were all about praising Jah Rastafari and being a Rasta man, or so they believed.

It had come to the point where I had to start taking responsibility for my own safety and wellbeing, to gain some wisdom and stop being so foolish.

I loved being natural and didn't like the thought of taking contraceptive pills. To me, those chemical medications were not natural to take and have in my system.

I have witnessed my mother take medication for years for her high blood pressure, and I didn't want that for my own inner-temple, but the final tipping point was my dreaded fear of falling pregnant by that man again.

Soon after Safiya's funeral, I made an appointment to see my doctor. He prescribed me contraceptive pills, and I began taking them, filled with overwhelming anxiety about getting pregnant again for that selfish and abusive bully. The fact that I had to take them in secret caused me endless months of fear and anxiety, in case he found out about it.

Life continued to be a hell on earth. He was ignorant in believing that he was always right, even when he was so wrong. His entitlement in believing that he was always right only served to give him an apparent sense of control and power to try to prove that everyone else, including me, was wrong. It was almost like an obsession of his, the need to always be right.

It was about a year later when I was rushed to hospital with a badly swollen leg. I was diagnosed with thrombosis; they found a clotting of the blood in the artery of my left leg. That and the swelling caused serious complications for my health, so they had to keep me in the hospital for several days to both observe and monitor my serious medical condition.

They insisted that I remain in the hospital bed the whole time as they were fearful the blood clot might move to another crucial part of my body, like my lungs, heart, or even my brain.

I didn't argue with them and did as I was told and stayed in the hospital bed. I didn't realise how critical and serious it was until the specialist doctor at City Road Hospital told me that he had no answers as to how I had survived as he had never seen a patient with such a massive amount of clotting who had survived and lived.

I knew it had to have been the Creator and my Guardian Angels who were protecting me. I knew my prayers had been heard and answered. For the first time, I felt that the Creator had a reason and purpose for keeping me alive.

Jeremiah 29 – Verse 11: 'For I know the plans I have for you, declares the Lord. Plans for your welfare and not for evil. To give you a future and hope.'

Even as my condition improved, I continued to pray for guidance and healing. I prayed some more for my Creator to show me my purpose in life, to show me the way. I cried almost every day and night because I could never *hear* the answers I sought.

There was one thing I knew for certain: Mr R *had* to go. My sanity was at stake. My home and my being had to be cleansed of all his evil, his negativity, and his abusive hate and mistreatment of me.

I began to take positive and active steps towards focusing and investing in my own wellbeing and spiritual growth. I read motivational books, like the one by Iyanla Vanzant called *Acts Of Faith*. Her written words helped to lift my spirits and my self-worth, and I learnt to stop blaming myself for the wrong others were doing to me. And yes, I prayed for that same individual, Mr R. I prayed to the Creator to give me the strength to carry on and to remove him from my life and my personal space. In my lowest moments, reading the book, *Acts of Faith*, kept me going and grounded. That book helped me to focus on my search for spiritual guidance, and I devoured every word written about understanding the imbalances that create stress in our lives, particularly within the relationships we have with ourselves and the world. I literally took those words and tried to apply them to my personal life, so I could begin to rebuild my self-esteem. That book would teach me to focus my thoughts and set goals with my intentions for each day.

It was only after I had been discharged from the hospital that I found out my condition had been caused by my doctor's prescribing me with a high dosage of the contraceptive. I tried to sue the doctor and the Louisa Road Health Centre, but unfortunately for me, they were successful in blocking my attempts and had somehow and conveniently lost my medical files, so in the end, I just gave up fighting the case.

It again forced me to look at my life and reflect on everything important to me. I made a promise to the Creator that I would do better. I cried tears of anguish and prayed for God to keep me alive to bring up my three surviving children: 'Please do not let me die, Lord. Help me to live so that I can nurture my children as I know that their father would not and could not look after them well. Give me the strength to carry on and to live a life filled with purpose.'

I still suffer from thrombosis today, after 26 years of first being diagnosed with the condition, but I am alive, even though I suffer daily.

The Lord knows that, in my heart, I have the utmost gratitude for His mercy in sparing my life so I could see my children and grandchildren flourish and grow.

That, alone, fills my heart with immense joy, happiness, and love.

Self-Help Tasks Towards Reflection and Inner Healing

- Have you ever experienced a deep loss?
  - How have your feelings for this loss evolved over time?
  - Write a minimum of 500 words detailing this traumatic life experience.

CHAPTER 10

The Day of Retribution

I took the step of banning Mr R from coming to the hospital, as he wanted to stop one of my male friends from visiting me. I was angered and aghast at his cheek and impudence; he who had considered it normal to embrace cheating as a way of life, with all of his lies and attempts at hiding his own infidelities.

At that stage, Mr R didn't know if I was going to live or die, but he had been more concerned and fixated on dictating to me which of my friends should be able to visit me or not!

Once the hospital had discharged me from their care, I went to stay with my friend June. We were similar in size, so she brought some of her clothes to the hospital for me, and I didn't inform Mr R of my discharge date. He only knew that I was out of the hospital when I returned to the house to collect my children and then returned to my friend's house.

He was embarrassed to know that I was more willing to stay with a friend than to come home, especially after having just recovered from such a serious illness. He had had no tolerance for my disobeying his orders or my willingness to resist his commands to do as he told me to do. He always showed signs of being a sore loser.

With my refusal to return home to him, he quieted down for a while.

As soon as I returned home, though, the abuse started up again, and his hyper-aggressiveness increased.

I called the police several times, to no avail.

I knew that I would eventually have to get rid of him once and for all. *Now, now. I don't mean that I planned to kill him!*

His day of retribution was soon upon him, and his punishment would be my vengeance, for the wrong he had inflicted upon me was coming closer to becoming a reality. I could no longer tolerate his conceit, arrogance, and compulsion to constantly give in to his selfish needs and willingness to disregard the needs or the safety of our children or me.

I swiftly and cautiously made plans for the children to go to their grandparents' house that weekend, as I knew there would be hell to pay for my having taken steps to remove him from my life, and I didn't want the children to witness any verbal or physically violent abuse that might occur.

I took the front door key out of his pocket as he slept peacefully, and in the dead of night, I packed up all of his belongings. The next morning, he predictably displayed his usual manner of rage when he realised that the front door key was missing from his pocket. In his aggressive state, he took the television and walked up the road with it, trying to goad me and upset me further. Instead, I calmly telephoned the police, and he dropped the television and fled!

Much later that evening, he returned and somehow managed to break into my house. I made sure to securely lock every door and window, so how he managed to break in was puzzling to me.

As I laid in bed that night, he stood over me in a threatening manner and hissed, 'Just to show you that I can get in here whenever I want to.'

I thought my life was going to end that night.

He grabbed me around the neck as he threatened me, and then he turned around and left the house. Even as he was squeezing the breath out of me, I determinedly chanted a prayer in my befuddled mind for God to protect me and keep me safe.

Psalms 23: 'The Lord is my Shepherd. I shall not want. He maketh me to lie down in green pastures. He leadeth me beside the still waters. He restoreth my soul, and He leadeth me in the paths of righteousness for His name's sake.'

Once again, I felt fearfully obliged to call the police, but by the time they arrived, he was nowhere to be found.

I honestly believed that somewhere inside of him, he had known that his vengeful, aggressive, abusive, and anti-social misbehaviour had been wrong and unacceptable, but yet, he felt comfortable with it because he felt I had wronged him by standing up to him. He had been angered by feeling that his dominance over me was slipping or was being ignored.

Finally, I found the courage to begin the process of taking out an injunction against him to prevent him from coming anywhere near me, my children, or my home. It wasn't easy bringing up three children, ages 9, 11, and 13 as a single mother.

Their father took no responsibility for their health, wellbeing, education, or financial support. He neglected their needs for a father's love and attention. For him to admit to a positive emotional feeling of any kind would mean or suggest that he could be affected by someone or something outside of his selfish, self-serving thoughts and needs.

My personal experiences taught me more than ever that some of these worthless and selfish men ought to be taught about taking accountability for their actions and how to honour their children and their children's lives.

1 Timothy 5 – Verse 8: 'But if anyone does not provide for his relatives and especially for members of his household, he has denied the faith and is worse than an unbeliever.'

The criticism I experienced from family members centred around their judgemental opinions regarding my children – how they thought my son was a bad boy and my daughter's way of expressing herself in a loud and vocal manner from a very early age was wrong and distasteful to their somewhat sensitive and delicate ears!

One thing I haven't forgotten to this day and which I've kept replaying in my mind was when my brother, Matthew, was getting married in Barbados. I remember working myself ragged to the point of exhaustion so I could save the fare for myself and my children to attend *his* wedding.

The very first thing that my brother commented to me upon meeting me at the airport was how he was dreading my children coming!

There were a few issues on the aeroplane as we flew to Barbados, so my daughter complained about it. My brother had misunderstood what was said and immediately started to moan about it. To this day, my children still talk about his unfair and judgemental reaction and his lack of a warm greeting after we had all made the effort to be there for him, to celebrate and support him with love on his wedding day.

I was so upset, and even more so that he had arranged transport for his wife to be's family members and not his own. Due to this lack of care, consideration, and respect for me and my children, I always said that one day he would have his own children and need many prayers that his upbringing of them would be a smooth ride. I wish him luck with that huge task as he, like many other parents, will need it.

For me, empowerment is never about blame. Empowerment is about taking personal responsibility, and that is what I decided to do, even when the father of my children refused to give me a penny to support his children.

I am a woman. I am a mother. I am a wife. I am not perfect. I have stretch marks on my stomach, and my breasts are no longer firm. Some days, I don't even want to do anything but to stay in my pyjamas all day. There are other days when I feel unstoppable. I have made a lot of mistakes in my life, and sometimes I may say the wrong things or choose the wrong life path to travel down. I stress over certain situations, incidents, or things. Sometimes I fret or stress over the little things in life, such as wanting those in my household to put the toilet seat down after they have used the bathroom. Other times I find myself stressing over past mistakes, like having chosen to love the wrong man.

My tears are mostly shed in private.

Sometimes, in my quiet moments, I laugh or smile at myself and my hidden vulnerabilities, as I am often perceived as 'Andrea, the strong, confident woman', so the public does not necessarily think or believe that I, too, can just as easily succumb to feeling low, tearful, sad, or even depressed.

I have a somewhat annoying tendency to procrastinate over things. On the other end of my characteristic scale, I am sometimes capable of taking positive action, of taking risks. I am not perfect, and my life, in general, is far from perfect, also.

I *know* that I have a 'calling'. I know that I have a purpose in life, which is to support other women who suffer from domestic violence and other kinds of personal abuse. I feel that I am a local and international voice for all vulnerable and abused women who suffer in silence.

I believe that through my personal, professional, and emotional growth as a result of the trauma and tragedies I have suffered in my life that I am a woman of empowerment and positive influence, striving to be happy and to be loved unconditionally.

TD Jakes once said, 'When you hold on to your history, you do it at the expense of your destiny.'

Self-Help Tasks Towards Reflection and Inner Healing

- Have you or a close loved one ever come close to having a near-death experience?

    - Did it have any lasting effect or impact on your thoughts, actions, and life?

Raising My Son as a Single Mother

I was consumed with worry and doubt about raising my son without a father.

Raising a child or children can be difficult under any circumstances, but without an involved and committed partner, the stakes feel higher, and the responsibility is far more worrying and heavily felt. The pressure, stress, and consequent fatigue is beyond belief and sometimes overwhelming.

I was intensely mindful of not making him feel like he had to be the man around the house and that he had the right to enjoy being a child. I had to learn to be creative when helping him to learn boys' stuff and make sure that his thought processes were honoured and listened to, as well.

Growing up in Aston in the 1990s where gangs were prevalent, I fretted constantly about how to keep my son out of these gangs, away from trouble, and out of prison.

I was mindful of being proactive in giving him books to read, books depicting and speaking highly of strong, Black men like Malcolm X, Marcus Garvey, and Martin Luther King.

I instilled positive quotes from those who had lived before us who had fought so valiantly to secure equal and just rights for all people of colour and humanity – all humanity – and not just the elite few in him. Many of these positive quotes, words, and thoughts I used to try to motivate and inspire him were from Malcolm X, Marcus Garvey, and Martin Luther King.

I wanted my son to know that he could be anything he wanted to be, and that hard work was worth every step of the way to his achieving his dreams, goals, and ambitions in life.

"Education is the passport to the future, for tomorrow belongs to those who prepare for it today.

"You are not so blind with patriotism that you cannot face reality. Wrong is wrong, no matter who does it or says it.

"There is no better than adversity. Every defeat, every heartbreak, every loss, contains its own seed, its own lessons on how to improve your performance the next time" **(Malcolm X).**

"A people without the knowledge of their past history, origin and culture, is like a tree without its roots.

"If you have no confidence in self, you are twice defeated in the race of life. With confidence, you have won even before you have started.

"Men who live their lives in earnest are not afraid of the consequences" **(Marcus Garvey).**

"Injustice anywhere is a threat to justice everywhere.

"Life's most persistent and urgent question is, what are you doing for others?

"I have decided to stick with love, for hate is too great a burden to bear.

"The true measure of a man is not where he stands in moments of comfort and convenience, but where he stands at times of challenge and controversy" **(Martin Luther King).**

I wanted to empower my son and instil in him a powerfully positive insight and understanding of great role models and leaders who looked like him. I wanted to ground him with a clear vision of what he could actively aspire towards in his own life. I kept him busy, ensuring he completed his school homework on time and way above the expected standard of the school's curriculum and expectations.

I made sure we enjoyed family days out and weekends to places like Cornwall, and as he was the only boy, he and my godson, Mathias, spent a lot of time together.

My son started to misbehave at school around the age of nine or ten, but we quickly established that he was extremely intelligent, completed his schoolwork quickly, and had too much spare time to fool around in class. His advanced intelligence meant he was moved up from Year 2 to Year 4, where he remained for two years. It was only much later that it came to light that the school, Manor Park School, could have sent my son to a Gifted Assisted Programme for gifted and talented children.

Thank you to the Head of Year teacher at that time for not giving my son that opportunity!

All through his childhood, I had to learn how to remain calm and not allow myself to give in to any of his emotional blackmail or pleas. I had to learn also how to put aside my personal loneliness in being a single parent to deal with this and any stress I encountered in our routine family life. I was hyper-sensitive, trying to be attuned to any feeling of loss he may have had or manifested.

I was determined to acknowledge the things he achieved with praise and encouragement. No matter what, I was determined to show him how much I loved him, and how much he was valued and respected, too.

I often wondered what goes on in a man's mind that he can walk away from his children and have no regard for their future upbringing or daily wellbeing and welfare. Mr R was supposed to have been there for his children to provide parental nurturing and guidance, but he totally abandoned them.

Ephesians 6:4 states: 'Fathers do not provoke your children to anger but bring them up in the discipline and instruction of the Lord.'

In knowing that I had to raise my son and other children as a single mother, I was intrigued to learn that if your child's biological father was emotionally, physically, or financially available and committed to your child then you were not considered a single mother, only a single woman!

I was definitely a single mother, then!

There were times when my son spoke to me as if he had no regard or respect for me as his mother, the person who had suffered sweat and tears to patiently and lovingly nurture his needs as a growing child. On the other hand, he could be the most loving and caring child and person toward me. During the times when he used to push me away or was disobedient, I had to be far more visibly and actively loving towards him. His display of disrespect towards me, his mother, a woman, illustrated a learnt male behaviour, passed down from grandfather, father, and then son.

Despite my leaving their violent and abusive father to give them a better and safer life, there were occasions when my son appeared to have no appreciation for what I had suffered, for his sake as well as my own. I worked hard to keep a roof over our heads, to feed my children, and to clothe them. I kept it basic in terms of teaching them fundamental manners and respect for life so they would grow to appreciate life with gratitude for the simple things in life.

In the past, I might have been guilty of not taking more time to show more love when I became the sole provider of our household and family. Growing up, I, too, had not been shown a great deal of tangible love from either of my parents. This was one aspect of female learnt behaviours that I was determined not to pass onto my children to the point at which it would impact their lives for years to come.

However, I am thankful and grateful that the foundations with which I equipped my son will allow him to be a better man and father than his or my previous generations. In my lowest moments, reading the book *Acts of Faith* kept me grounded in my faith and belief that all would be well in the end. This book helped me to focus on my search for spiritual guidance so I could pass these lessons onto my son for him to gift his own children.

From somewhere deep within me, I found the patience and the means to build him up and remind him that I would always be there for him. The hearts and minds of children can be so fragile at times, and I did not want to be responsible for shattering or breaking his heart, mind, or soul beyond repair.

I had no wish to burden him or any of my other children with my daily struggle regarding finances, emotions, or battling with social interactions.

Some positive aspects of being a single mother meant that I could dedicate my time to my children without the negative distraction of dealing with an abusive partner and that in time, my children and I developed a shared friendship and respect that would endure from their childhood into adulthood. From a very young age, they had to learn the importance of the responsibility of self and for those who were always there for them.

It can be seriously hard being a single mother, and it is often seen as a thankless and lonely job that you do alone. Sometimes, it doesn't matter the reason why, as very often, people do not care, and you will still be stigmatised, regardless.

Not only was it my responsibility to nurture my children, to help them with their homework, and to play with them, but it was also vital that I cultivated their emotional intelligence, as well.

Being a single parent, despite its hardships, gave me the chance to develop stronger bonds with my children and spend quality time with them. For that, I will always be grateful.

Of course, there are many reasons for women to become single mothers, like divorce, break-up, or death. Unfortunately, in my case, the need and necessity to escape an abusive and increasingly dangerous situation was my primary reason.

I had now reached a pinnacle time in my life where I need to put myself first.

The Creator is the representation of the good in my life, so, therefore, I must be good to me.

I need to find ways to keep myself spiritually, emotionally, physically, and mentally well to keep myself whole and holy so that others could not come into my life to try to steal or mess with the positive energy I needed for myself.

As Martin Luther King said, "Freedom is never voluntarily given by the oppressor. It must be demanded by the oppressed."

Self-Help Tasks Towards Reflection and Inner Healing

- What is the most challenging and/or rewarding situation you have had to face regarding your child or children?

  - In doing so, did you have to face and overcome fears, prejudices, tears, and/or phobias?

CHAPTER 12

My Soul Mates

I had another *brother*, my soulmate. His name was Charles. We may not have been blood-related, but he was my brother from another mother, as the saying goes.

He fancied me from the age of 14. Charles was spontaneous and funny, and he made me laugh. He loved being adventurous and was always a very loyal and dear friend.

He was someone to whom I could talk. He looked after me like a solid, reliable, and loving bigger brother would. He called my mother 'Mum,' and he loved and respected women.

He lived in Birmingham before moving to London, partly to escape certain personal and distressing issues regarding the mothers of his babies. However, he always maintained contact with me, and whenever there was an issue or crisis unfolding in my roller-coaster of a life, he appeared by my side like my guardian angel.

He always held on to the desire and hope that we would get married one day, but in my eyes, that would not have been ethical or right as I knew both of his baby-mothers, and we all got on so well, so I had no qualms or difficulty in keeping my dignity and self-respect on that score.

Charles always expressed his disgust at the way Mr. R the father of my children treated me, and he always wanted to rescue me, like my knight in shining armour. Unfortunately, his deepest wish behind wanting to save me wasn't to be, as life was too complicated and chaotic for me at that time.

My other soulmate, Rick, is the humblest and most loving man I have ever met. I cannot remember where we met, but they do say that people come into your life for a reason, a season, or a lifetime. Well, he has been in my life for a lifetime, and we have loved each other from near and far. I just couldn't allow myself to get too close to him as I felt it would be truly unfair as he had no children of his own, and I really wanted him to have his own children, and I already had all the children I wanted and needed. I vowed to myself a very long time ago that I would only have children from one man, even though that one man, the father of my children, had treated me so dreadfully and abusively.

When I was getting married, I invited Rick, but in my heart, I knew he wouldn't come. How could he attend and voicelessly witness me giving my heart to another man? Rick knew my deepest thoughts, my heart, and he understood my life. I couldn't blame him for not coming, so I had to respect his wishes to decline the invitation. We are still firm friends to this day.

Matthew also lived in Birmingham, and he moved to London, mainly due to his disorderly lifestyle involving the women in his life. We met in the city of Birmingham at the FCF, a nightclub in Handsworth. Entry to the club was only about £2 for the night, back in those days, and you could party in the room at the top of the club till the late morning hours, especially on Friday nights. I remember the FCF Club always had a lovely atmosphere.

As it turned out, I had had to end *that* relationship before it even really began. I felt that I was in love with him, but I hadn't been prepared to share his love with his baby-mothers and a dozen or so children resulting from his liaison with these numerous other women.

I resorted to writing him a long letter severing our relationship, and then I walked away from the potential and problematic possibilities of that love affair.

I just couldn't risk becoming too attached to him emotionally, knowing that he wasn't a free man who could love me back the way I needed loving. I needed something far more permanent in my life than a man who wasn't free to be with me all the time.

And who was to say that I wouldn't end up being one of his many women friends with benefits? Where would he find the time or energy to treat me right and be there for me when I needed him the most?

Then there was Mr T, the one I thought with whom I would never part – the married man. Our love was so intense, passionate, and full-on.

My ten year-long affair with Mr T, the married man, had had its highs and lows, as one would expect.

I once heard someone say that a married man chases after having sexual relationships with other women so they can try to regain or recapture some of the romance, attention, and passionate sex that is missing from their relationships with their wives, that they use other women – affairs – as a temporary means to fulfil their unfulfilled desires and wishes.

When you think about it deeply, an affair with a married man might be because of his selfish interests, which could only mean unnecessary complications for me, so I had to cut that short before I was hurt too badly all over again.

I had enough trauma and drama to deal with in my life, and eventually, the affair became a part of the problem for me. I think that, in the end, I became more emotionally insecure, doubting my sense of self, and questioning everything about me and around me. I also believe that there is a huge emotional difference, as a woman, in being the 'other' as opposed to being the 'significant other' when having an intimate relationship with a married man.

Despite the many highs, that affair did nothing to enhance my lack of trust in others.

Even though it was possible to love someone who was cheating on his wife with you, it didn't necessarily mean that he was a bad person, either, but over time, it was proven and shown to me that he couldn't have known much about what love really was.

Could it be that cheaters are really and truly just insecure because they hadn't experienced love or being wanted during their formative years?

Despite the initial and ongoing thrill of being a part of that affair, there were times where I felt anxious, guilty, ashamed, worried, regretful, and confused. There may have even been times when I felt self-loathing, too.

Psychologically, there must have been times when my inner silenced rage and thoughts of betrayal affected me mentally and emotionally. My self-image felt like it had been somehow damaged.

Surely, cheating indicated a lack of open communication between him and his wife, and therefore, it would follow that, in time, that same lack of honest and open communication would apply to him and me.

It hurt me a great deal to walk away at the time, but time itself is a great healer.

Self-Help Tasks Towards Reflection and Inner Healing

- Do you have a soulmate in your life, someone you feel spiritually and unconditionally connected to?

  – What do you feel both of you have in common that creates the bond between you?

CHAPTER 13

Reclaiming My Self-Empowerment

I knew and dreaded, that for me to find my voice, to tell my story, I had to become *visible*.

I had to learn how to evolve to become the positive and empowered woman I knew that I could be. I could no longer secretly hold on to my personal history. I had to find some way of being comfortable in stepping out after my having suffered in silence for so long so I could finally speak my truth. I had to find a way to break the chain of suffering and accepting the abusive behaviour without having questioned it. I had to be the strong woman within my own family.

To do so, I had to first forgive my ancestors, my father, the father of my own children, and the abused women in my family.

I also had to learn to forgive myself.

I had free myself from my past, to let go of it so I could then move on and look forward to a more positive future. I wanted to be free from the destructive patterns of behaviour that kept me down and as if feeling the worst was all I deserved in life.

I had this deep desire to get to a point where I could align myself with my purpose in life, to be true to myself and take responsibility for my actions and whatever happened to me.

I longed to live my life with and in truth and love, with grace and forgiveness.

I knew it would take time, but I am well on my way to living my life and embracing a life of fullness, and I am no longer afraid to honour myself as a woman, a mother, a daughter, or a person of worth and love.

Through my life's journey, I learnt that my true empowerment is *within* me. My Creator lives within me and always has, which enables me to anchor my divine truth in everything I think, say, and do. For me to genuinely re-empower myself, I had to get to that point in my life where I could represent myself, my interests, and my purpose in a responsible and self-determined way. I needed to be accountable for my past, present, and future. I needed to take control of my life, set realistic goals, and make positive decisions. I had to reach that place where I had a deeper understanding of my strengths and weaknesses and believe in who I was and who I could be.

When living my purpose in life, I want to reach out to people on a global level, sharing with them all of my wisdom in a genuine way whilst creating and building my own unique brand of who I am and what I do and have to offer others. I want to help abused women, to show them a way of how the y, too, can re-empower themselves towards healing and never having to be fearful or afraid ever again. I want to show other women that it is achievable, to be open to all possibilities, and to focus on who they were, to trust themselves and to love themselves whilst holding themselves in grace.

I want to reach out to people from all walks of life with my true and flawed self. I want to create a unique brand to help vulnerable women regain their sense of power and follow their truths. I want them to find their purpose in life so they can recognise the early warning signs of unacceptable behaviour in their personal and social relationships. I want them to know that it is not healthy, and they have the choice to get out as soon as possible, so they don't prolong their suffering.

People view me as strong, independent, motivated, and confident. They see me as someone who believes in herself. I *am* all that, but at times, when I was going through my own experiences of hurt and pain, I would have loved for someone to have taken my hand and tell me that everything was going to be okay. I was so lost, and I needed to be found.

We all have one life, and we have the right to choose how we want to live it without harming another person or ourselves.

We shouldn't live our lives with regret, apologising for wanting better or hating ourselves because somebody else has made us feel so worthless.

We shouldn't be living our lives with regret for not having done the things we wanted to do, or we wanted to be. Do what is best for you as an individual by taking risks, living life to the fullest, and loving without fear.

I grew up watching my father abuse my mother physically, mentally, and financially. I am not sure what she ever wanted out of life for herself. Had she wanted to be heard? To be loved and respected? All I ever saw was a very unhappy woman who had no life of her own. I felt that I had more freedom and independence than she ever did. I was able to go to college, work, and travel to other countries.

There were times when I could see how my behaviour and my character mirrored my mother's submissiveness through fear and a lack of self-worth. I, too, had been silently crying out for help, suffering behind closed doors. I wonder if my mother had any regret over what she endured for all those years.

I can understand why, in *Corinthians 6 Verse 14*, it says, '*Be ye not unequally yoked together with unbelievers: for what fellowship hath righteousness and unrighteousness and what communion hath light with darkness?*'

As women, we need to wise up and take ownership of who we are and that which we represent or that for which we stand.

A man who cannot lead you in prayer cannot lead you in your personal life.

I do not think that I have ever seen my father lead in prayer, so my mother was always and will always live in a hopeless situation, ever hoping to find happiness at the core of their marital union; it will continue to be her light against the darkness. The only comfort I feel in my heart for my mother is in knowing that her unshakeable faith in God affords her a depth of love and acceptance that she clings to and has faith unto this day. Therein, I believe, lies her true joy in life.

As women of worth, we must honour ourselves not to allow other people to drag us from where God has brought us, from an inner-light and a soul that deserves to be loved and treated well.

Real Kings are never afraid to show affection, devotion, respect, and love to and for their Queens. They will protect, provide, and live with the intention of pleasing and uplifting their Queens, their partners, their wives.

A woman should always feel excited to see her *King*, the one who consistently and affectionately nurtures her with love and attention and treats her right. Love is not always about what you say, but it is about what you *do*.

As my mother endured for years, myself and my precious daughter.

We all need to be accountable when it comes to breaking the curse of this vicious and life-threatening cycle.

Whenever we find ourselves submerged in loveless relationships, we are surrounded by engulfing darkness and only an inner-light of hope can bring into the relationship that which we should ultimately have and nurture within ourselves, first and foremost. Darkness cannot drive out darkness, so if we continue to live in destructive relationships, it will be difficult and sometimes impossible for that light to shine or even for it to ignite.

Yes, I know that sometimes we need to go through the storms, fires, and tribulations of life to reach our ultimate purpose and destiny in life, but still, I continue to question the *why* of this!

I get so angry at times, and this is due to so many things that gradually built up inside of me over so many years, things that inevitably brought me to tears and an almost bitter anger. It is an anger to which I tended to cling for too long (and to which I still cling) and of which I must finally learn to let go. Letting go is so hard when it is all that you have known and taken some perverse comfort in because the alternative is far too scary to experience.

The hurtful words spewed out in anger towards us as victims of abuse and the unfortunate way we take those damaging words for truth only serves to make us sick physically, mentally, emotionally and spiritually.

Any kind of abuse perpetrated against us is not love – it is hatred and disrespect at its deepest and rawest level.

Our men and partners need to realise that their words and self-obsessed and negatively harmful actions do have a far-reaching impact on our mental and emotional wellbeing. They need to realise that life, in general, is not always about them, and that life doesn't always revolve around them and their egotistical needs and wants. They must learn not to emote their negative feelings onto others in such a dreadful and harmful way.

For those on the receiving end of being abused in any way, shape, or form, this is the reason why personal self-care is so important and necessary. Our health is our wealth, so we cannot afford to lose our internal peace when trying to '*fix*' an abusive or narcissistic partner.

Loyalty and trust is vital in every relationship, so if your man wants to disrespect a woman, I suggest that he write it down in black and white and present it to his mother, so that his mother will be aware of the sordid and hateful things he has said to those he should be treating like a Queens. Words like *whore* and *nasty bitch* only serve to illustrate their lack of self-worth and integrity for themselves and all the women they abuse. It demonstrates how they do not and cannot love women. If they loved and respected women, they – the men – would not choose to have such demeaning thoughts, much less use these derogatory and hurtful words. Their thoughts and behaviours are based purely on personal gain and inflated egos and not on any level of decent values.

Self-empowerment is about having the ability to do something about your personal needs or learning how to do something about your personal needs, wants, opinions, beliefs, and feelings.

Personal empowerment is all about having a collection of beliefs, actions, and skills, all of them working together to create a life that can be lived with awareness and positivity.

As a woman who was once a victim of abuse and violence, I had to learn ways to re-educate myself to become a strong presence and show up as a woman who survived and overcame with perseverance, determination, courage, and integrity.

Empowerment is more about actions than feelings. It is more a reflection of our increased personal values and self-worth that grows out of our life experiences and lessons learnt, of having real influence in one or more areas of our lives.

Learning how to use empowerment skills to benefit me in a positive way, including coping, intellectual, and communicative skills. This includes communicating with myself and my thoughts.

In reclaiming my self-empowerment, words like passionate, wellness, renewal, thriving, purposeful, courage, hope, love, and self-worth became more and more a part of my natural, daily vocabulary.

CHAPTER THIRTEEN: RECLAIMING MY SELF-
EMPOWERMENT

Self-Help Tasks Towards Reflection and Inner Healing

- Self-empowerment – what does this mean to you personally?

- Write a piece illustrating how powerless you felt. Describe the circumstances and how you overcame the situation.

CHAPTER 14

I Am a Survivor

I survived 13 years of abuse by my children's father, Mr R, and had to overcome immense challenges and adversities.

I had reached the point where I was on a mission to pursue, restore, and transform my life to enable me to remain sane for my children's sake, and strive not to bring that toxic and destructive baggage into my present – now, recently past – relationship and marriage.

I worked extremely hard to remove myself from being an abused, unemployed, struggling, single mother to becoming a wife, a master health coach, the founder of Embrace Health and Wellbeing CIC, and supporting vulnerable and abused women within our communities. KAMJERSARA – which I named after my three children – it is both a De-Cluttering Service, which helps hoarders clear and organise their homes and my events management business, where I provide the professional and personal service of decorating halls and venues for weddings, birthday parties, events, and such.

I had to learn how to retrain my brain to stop listening to all the negative thoughts seeping through, especially during my lowest moments. It was not easy, as I was already entrenched into listening to it for years, and most tragically, believing every word. I had to redefine myself and learn how to recognise and acknowledge my true purpose in life, my empowerment as a woman, my uniqueness, my capacity for self-love, my bliss, and my joy.

I feel that I still have a long way to go, but I know that, by the grace of the Creator, I will get there because I now feel unstoppable, far stronger, and I refuse to carry on, suffering in silence.

It is important to remember that not all abuse is physical. Emotional, financial, and mental abuse is equally devastating and isolating for those who suffer it in silence.

Self-Help Tasks Towards Reflection and Inner Healing

- Do you feel that you have survived an abusive period in your personal or professional life?
  - What pivotal moment do you think occurred to enable you to survive, keep going, and escape?

CHAPTER 15

How I Got My Groove Back

After courageously freeing myself from Mr R's detrimental clutches and abuse, I made a vow to myself that I would never again live with another man unless I were married to him.

I met a man, who I call Mr T, through a mutual male friend (the same married man I spoke about earlier). At that time, I was feeling quite good about myself; I felt free and happy, at last. I was even going out clubbing every weekend, something I hadn't really done in the past, but I had found a new lease on life and freedom.

My friend Dee and I went out on Friday nights to The Barrel Pub, then on to Tobasco's, situated on Heathfield Road, on Saturday nights. Sundays, we would make our way to Thasher's, which was located on Soho Road in Handsworth.

I noticed how my life began to change simply because I had finally learnt how to alter my mindset and my way of thinking. I knew that I needed to change my thoughts, the way I spoke, and how I conducted myself.

Finally, I began to feel a level of happiness that had been missing previously from my life. I felt happy, loved, and respected, however this man with whom I was involved, happened to be a *married* man.

We did so much together. We drank Champagne, ate at expensive restaurants, pampered ourselves at various spas, and enjoyed basking in the warm waters of a Jacuzzi and relaxing in the sauna on a Sunday afternoon. I felt I was almost in my element. It felt good, but again, I was living and suffering in silence. This time, it was the silence created by being intimately involved with a married man.

I wouldn't dare tell anyone my huge secret, even though it felt exciting, as if I were living on the edge of something sweet and great.

I couldn't help but feel a sense of guilt that I – Andrea, the woman with such high morals and personal integrity was a mistress. It felt great at that time and only a few of my closest friends knew my secret.

I felt great because I could put on my sexy underwear most weekends as the children were away at their grandparents.

He drove a soft-top BMW, which I thought was the be-all-and-end-all of sophistication, and I *felt* happy.

There were still sporadic and violent outbursts I had to endure from my ex-partner once he found out about my new relationship. He came around to vandalise my car, breaking the aerial or maliciously keying it to damage the paintwork. Because of this, I had to resort to taking out another injunction against him to keep him away from me and my property.

My clandestine, intimate relationship ended after ten long years as I felt we were not growing as individuals or as a couple, and my children were growing up by themselves. Life was not always about just having fun, and I strongly felt that I needed to be a role model and set a good example for my children at the end of the day.

The time had come when I had to finally be brutally honest with myself as well as with him, but in hindsight, he should have had the courage and self-respect to have made the decision to leave his wife or not.

When we parted ways, we were still deeply in love.

Despite this *love* we felt for each other during our ten-year relationship, both his wife and another, younger girl had given birth to a child by him. Regarding the other lady, my family knew her family very well, but I will not mention names. At the time, I still didn't really care as long as it wasn't me that was pregnant as I was enjoying life, having fun, and feeling free as the birds in the trees. I even told him not to worry about me but to be more concerned about when his wife found out that he had impregnated another woman!

My children had grown to love him, too, as he was the complete opposite of their violent and abusive father.

Mr. T was placid, humble, loving, caring and thoughtful – everything a woman could ask for. He was even very good in bed, and I had no cause for any complaints with him in that department.

Like I said, the relationship continued for ten years. I was 30 years of age when we first met, and as beautiful as it had felt to me, I knew that I had to end it because I knew in my heart that, one day, karma would return to bite me on the butt.

I was at a stage in my life where I was growing more on a personal level, reading more insightful literature, and embracing my life experiences with more clarity.

In my quest for personal and spiritual growth, Iyanla Vanzant was one of the authors I followed faithfully. *One Day My Soul Just Opened Up* was one of her books that I read. I had no idea that, in the years to come, I would eventually be presented with the opportunity to meet Iyanla Vanzant in person. It was when I had travelled to the Hackney Theatre with a good friend of mine and the Shakti Women, a Black women's organisation based in Birmingham. We arrived at the theatre in a limousine, and our VIP tickets meant that we were fortunate enough to have access to meet her backstage.

After ending that relationship with the married man, I met and linked up with a bad boy named Ren who worked in security, but the story of that encounter is possibly another book!

Having read the book *One Day My Soul Just Opened Up*, I fasted and prayed for 40 days and nights in 1995, and it helped to reveal to me that bad boy REN I had been seeing in London during that time no longer served my present or future purpose in life. His drug-dealing, fornication, and life of guns were not for me, so he could no longer be an integral part of my future life.

I was immensely grateful to the Creator for showing me that I needed to end that relationship and for guiding me back to a right and meaningful track of life and inner-happiness.

I could so easily have ended up dead or imprisoned, just as another woman with whom he had been having an affair; she wound up doing time in prison.

I had to quickly learn how to break away from what was no longer good for me or which no longer served my purpose.

A spirit of discernment and good instincts are priceless gifts in being able to distinguish, judge, or appraise another person occupying space in your life.

In the New Testament, it describes 'the ability to distinguish between spirits' as in 1 Corinthians 12:20 and to discern good and evil as in Hebrews 5:14 (www.spiritualgiftstest.com).

I was fast learning that you can only be abusively violated if you allow someone to do it to you.

I am also learning to be unapologetic for who I am and that for which I stand. Some people who did not know me very well would make statements saying that I think am too nice and that I am so full of myself. To them, I say, Yes! I am nice. I am beautiful. I am blessed with the confidence of self. I am unstoppable, and my cup is full and spills over with life's blessings.

I am trying each day just to be the best version of me that I possibly can be.

I know that my life will continue to evolve and improve, and I cannot wait to share my gifted greatness with the world.

Many of us have been through things that have been so traumatic, things for which the human mind was not necessarily built to handle, but we fight and persevere every single day and night. If that is not inner-strength, I don't know what is.

We are beautiful survivors, Queens with a purpose in life.

Self-Help Tasks Towards Reflection and Inner Healing

- In what ways do you feel you have rediscovered your 'groove'?

  - In writing about this, do you feel that certain thoughts, actions, or emotions, helped in your rediscovery?

- If you are presently looking to find the 'new you' and to 'Get Your Groove Back' some activities I suggest are:
  - Dancing
  - Joy
  - Laughter
  - Reading
  - Relaxation
  - Self-focus
  - Creativity
  - Overcoming your fears

- What other activities can you list to help you get your groove back?

Acknowledgements

In acknowledging the following persons, I would like to personally thank them, also.

I would like to express my deepest appreciation to my Mother, my Queen, my heartbeat, my love, who gave me the inspiration, the courage, and the strength to write this book in the hope of changing and saving lives. Your love and support encouraged me in wanting to help women to see that abuse can happen to anyone, to ordinary people like you and me. I wanted to break the cycle of this generation. In sharing my story, it has taught me how to own my inner light and how to rise from this generational curse that has held us, as a family, to ransom, for too many years. I needed to see a positive transformation within our family and Mum, I did this for you, myself and for our future generations. I love you.

I would like to extend my sincere gratitude to Maxine Palmer-Hunter, for being there for me, for being such a good listener. You have been my rock, a friend who I know always has my back and who never lets me down. I am deeply indebted to you as you have never once wavered in your support of and for me. Maxine and Dan Palmer-Hunter. Thank you both for being there when no-one else was there for me. You are such a great example of what true friendship looks and feels like. Your undeniable integrity and love and support of me has instilled in me a lasting self-belief that I will always be grateful for. I will always love you both.

I would like to acknowledge my three children, Sara, Kamilah and Jermaine, who have given me the strength to carry on when times were so bad that I had felt like giving up. You all were the reasons that I felt I had to live to look after you all and that has been my joy, my sources of love, my life, and my light. I am forever grateful to you all, my beautiful children.

I want to thank all those who took the time to write their reviews for my book. I will always be humbly grateful to you all. Thank you to Maxine Palmer-Hunter, Vanessa Nova-Oviasu, Paulette Hamilton, Sara Maynard, to name a few. Thank you for reading my story in advance and for the lovely words each of you have written in support of me and my personal story.

I would like to acknowledge my former husband Joe, for the thirteen years we shared and for all the wonderful things we did together. I thank you for the love that we once shared and despite each of us now going our separate ways, I wish you well as I step into a life of learning to love myself with the depth and respect, I so deserve.

I would like to acknowledge Deborah Lovell, my cousin, who I owe a world of gratitude to, for being so lovingly present in supporting me during the good and bad times. You have been consistent in supporting and nurturing me and in keeping me sane. Thank you for being my therapist, my healer, and my friend. I very much appreciate you.

To the Kings and Queens, those groups of friends who kept my spirits uplifted. Thank you for the many holidays abroad to Barbados, Jamaica, Gambia, Cuba, Mexico and so many other destinations, too many to mention here. Thank you for those wonderful day trips to Royal Ascot, the birthday celebrations, the times we met up and enjoyed eating meals out together, the various trips to the theatres, the parties, clubbing and the enjoyment we experienced at Carnivals.

I acknowledge with love, my sister, Doreen Maynard, who was always ready to share wise words of wisdom with me, without judgement. You provided that listening ear that was so important to me then and now. I thank you sincerely for your honesty and utmost respect in dealing with my situations and with me, especially at a time when I needed you the most.

I would like to extend my gratitude to Danni Blechner and her team, Elise Abram, my editor and Oksana Kosovan, my typesetter at at Conscious Dreams Publishing for their combined works and final finessing of my book manuscript so that my dreams of having my book published could become a reality. Thank you all.

Finally, I would like to thank my Book Manuscript Editor, siSTAR Maureen Elizabeth Worrell, without whom the completion of this book, *Suffering In Silence*, would not have been possible. Without you Maureen, this story would not have been written so that I could share it with the world. You have been so very instrumental in the achievement of this goal and I am extremely grateful to you for all your hard work and all those times you worked throughout the night to meet our deadlines. Thank you for encouraging me to step into my courage and to know that I have a voice that is worthy of being heard through my written words and for believing that my story will serve to inspire others to speak out and to be heard also. I am grateful also for your passion and dedication in wanting to help victims and survivors of domestic violence and abuse to heal mentally and emotionally. Blissings in abundance.

We need to know that we are all destined with the potential of greatness and that we share our stories to let others know we can overcome.

About the Author

Andrea Maynard-Brade is a British writer and businesswoman, Complimentary Therapist and Master Coach born to Caribbean parents.

She is respected for her positive influence and purposefulness in working with vulnerable women towards rebuilding their confidence and self-esteem as well as offering them support to regain their health and wellbeing. She spends a vast amount of her time contributing to community developments and health awareness. She teaches self-empowerment to overcome life's challenges.

Suffering In Silence epitomises her struggles and her experiences in how she overcame a life beset with numerous incidences of domestic abuse and violence, sexual assault, and the tragic loss of her baby to stillbirth. It also illustrates how she emerged from victim to victorious, a woman re-empowered with a purpose in life to helping others.

She is the Founder of Positive Mouves Holistic and Training and EMBRACE Health and Wellbeing CIC. She is also the proud CEO of KAMJERARA – De-Cluttering Service, which helps hoarders clear and organise their homes and an interior design company that caters for weddings and which she named after her children. She is also a trained Master Holistic Health Coach and Reiki Master and co-founder of Black Women in Business.

Her previous writings have appeared in 'Pain to Purpose' and 'The Book of Inspiration for Women by Women'.

In 2015 she was the recipient of the Women of Power and Influence Award and in 2016, she won the EMBRACE and BEXLIVE Health and Wellbeing Awards. In 2017 she was awarded the Ambassador Award for her contributions to the Universal Peace Federation.

Contact the Author

You can contact Andrea at:

@embrace.elevate.luv

Andrea Maynard-Brade

Embrace-HealthWellbeing-CIC

embracehw@gmail.com

Conscious Dreams
PUBLISHING

Be the author of your own destiny

Find out about our authors, events, services
and how you too can get your book journey started.

 Conscious Dreams Publishing

 @DreamsConscious

 @consciousdreamspublishing

 Daniella Blechner

 www.consciousdreamspublishing.com

 info@consciousdreamspublishing.com

Let's connect

Lightning Source UK Ltd.
Milton Keynes UK
UKHW020630090421
381705UK00006B/197

9 781913 674458